IN THE
CRUCIBLE

IN THE CRUCIBLE

*'Unless a grain of wheat falls
to the ground and dies,
it remains only a single seed.
But if it dies, it produces many seeds.'*

Robert Warren

HIGHLAND BOOKS

DEDICATION

To my father,
Peter Warren.

ISBN 0 946616 54 X

Cover design: Diane Drummond, Words & Images

Printed in Great Britain for
HIGHLAND BOOKS
Broadway House, The Broadway,
Crowborough, East Sussex TN6 1BY
by Richard Clay Ltd, Bungay
Typeset by Harperset, Maidstone

CONTENTS

INTRODUCTION

I have spent ten years resisting invitations to write this book. I am glad to have done so. There is certainly more of a story to tell. But there is another reason for being glad to have delayed writing. Those ten years have given me a fresh perspective on success and failure in the Christian life.

'Success' is a word that most Christians fight shy of. Certainly our calling is to something different from worldly success; yet scripture is full of stories of ways in which God has given success to his people. The mission of Jesus is the supreme model for us in this. I have been prompted to think about why and how some aspects of the life of St Thomas's have gone well and borne fruit. Those thoughts are largely expressed in some of the 'theory' chapters that are scattered through the book. In these chapters I have sought to get at some of the underlying principles that have guided our actions.

Those principles, hammered out on the anvil of experience, have a more enduring quality than the particular practices through which they are expressed in our situation at present. My understanding is that how we got where we did is of more value to others than the actual destination. Not that we, or any church, ever arrives. The Christian life is a pilgrimage (on the Way) and there is always more to learn. There is also often a battle to hold on to what we have learnt and to avoid living on past reputation rather than present reality.

'Failure' also has a distinctively Christian form. One of the chief conclusions I have come to about our experience of God has been that true effectiveness in the kingdom of God grows out of going the way of the Cross. Again and again we have found that the point of struggle, despair, weakness, failure and pain have been — in the purposes of God — the seedbed of later fruitfulness. It is that sense of being in a crucible of God's choosing, while he — often painfully — works on his church to purify and refine it that is expressed not just in the title but in the story.

This story could not have been told if it were not for the hundreds of people who have played a part in it. Only a few have been mentioned by name; they have been singled out simply as living illustrations of what many others were doing in a hidden but vital way. I want to acknowledge those many unnamed members of the church who have played vital parts in this story.

I have mentioned most of the nine churchwardens I have been privileged to work with. They have consistently been such a support to me, and worked incredibly hard in the Lord's vineyard usually after long days at their own responsible jobs. They have always been patient with me, and loving enough to tell me when I have been wrong. Without the confidence I have had in them there would have been so much less risk, and so much less story. Two in particular, Terry Pratt and Richard Laughlin, have given valuable help with the writing of this book.

My wife, Ann, has played a great part in this story. There is no ministry without sacrifice. Ann has been willing to forego her preference for a quiet and ordered life, as well as being willing for me to be out at all hours of the day and night. Her temperament and way of seeing things is so different from mine and has been like a second pair of eyes. Without her ability to see through to the heart of situations and to face me with reality there would have been much less of a story to tell. Her down-to-earth approach has kept my feet on the ground. When everything has gone wrong she has reminded me of the scripture that 'Though all is dark and there is no light, yet will I trust Thee' (Isaiah 50.10). When things have gone well I have reminded myself of the remark of the wife of the former Canadian Prime Minister, Lester Pearson, who said, 'Behind every great man, there stands an astonished woman.'

Yet the true honour goes to the army of church members who, as the people of God, have been willing to go through a series of crucible experiences, and have been so responsive to such leadership as I have exercised. Time and time again I have marvelled at their sacrifice and willingness to follow some of the crazy ways that we have been.

Above all, this is a story about God and his grace and surprises. It is his story and to him alone the glory is due. It has been, and remains, a privilege to be part of his purposes. My prayer is that our story and the lessons we have learnt will help other churches to find God's presence and his way for them. May his grace be seen and multiplied through this story.

DIARY OF EVENTS

Jul 1964 .... Michael Cole instituted as vicar.
May1967 .... Second morning service started.
Jan 1971 .... Michael Cole's farewell service.
Apr 1971 .... Robert Warren instituted as vicar.
Oct 1971 .... Two morning services reformed into
.... one service at 10.30am.
Mar 1972 .... Jean Darnall preaches.
Oct 1972 .... Operation Eyesore gift day.
Apr 1973 .... David Hughes begins as curate.
Mar 1974 .... Idea of supporting fellowships shared
.... at church weekend at Whirlow Grange.
Jul 1974 .... Gifts gift day.
Nov 1975 .... Conception of re-building idea.
Jan 1977 .... Robert Potter appointed as architect.
Jan 1977 .... Valedictory service for Patrick & Gill
.... Coghlan and last service in the 'old'
.... St Thomas's.
Jan 1977 .... First service for St Thomas's in Crookes
.... Baptist Church.
Jun 1979 .... Building work began.
Dec 1980 .... Last Sunday at Crookes Baptist Church.
Dec 1980 .... Re-opening service of the new St Thomas's.
Aug 1982 .... Joint morning services with Anglicans
.... and Baptists began.
Sep 1982 .... Crookes Endowed Centre opened.
Oct 1982 .... Your Kingdom Come: service to mark the
.... inauguration of the local ecumenical project.
Jun 1983 .... Finishing the Task gift day. (£27,000).
Jan 1984 .... Council decides to reduce staff team by

Chapter One

NOTHING TO SET BEFORE THEM

I was in no mood for a challenge.

That morning I had come out of Wolverhampton General Hospital after recovering from a severe attack of meningitis. My wife, Ann, had come to collect me, and on our return home we opened the post. It included a letter from the Church Pastoral Aid Society inviting me to consider the post of vicar of St Thomas's, Crookes, in Sheffield. One of the things a new incumbent would be expected to tackle was a major building project. It was the last thing I wanted.

After ordination I had worked as a curate to Michael Baughen at Holy Trinity, Platt, in Manchester. It had been a marvellous, and exhausting, start to my ministry. We had seen God at work in many ways. People came to faith, and the church had grown significantly. Having responsibility for an after-church Sunday evening meeting which drew hundreds, and for a youth group which grew from six to sixty, I had been able to learn from an outstanding leader. My sights of what a church could become had been set high.

I had watched as Michael Baughen led the church into a major building project in which he was

hammering out the faith principles that have since
been applied by many others across the country. I
was aware of the enormous workload such a
venture involved and was not at all sure I wanted to
go that way — unless I had to.

However, Michael had been the one through
whom so much had happened. When the time came
to move, I needed most of all to find out if God
would turn up when only Robert Warren was there.

St James's, Fordhouses, in Wolverhampton had
certainly given us that opportunity. Sometimes it
really did seem as if only Robert and Ann Warren
were there. A new dual-purpose building had been
put up eighteen months before. All it lacked was a
congregation. We inherited a morning congregation that every now and then reached double
figures. By the time we left, the building was full to
overflowing with over two hundred people of all
ages crammed in for the monthly family services.
We had even applied the faith principles I learnt in
Manchester and found God faithful. The first gift
day had a target of one hundred pounds. Minuscule
though that now sounds, it was a leap of faith for a
church at the end of the 1960s. The total income of
the church in the previous year had been less than
that. Ann and I saw God at work in that hidden
corner. We both cut our teeth and learnt many
lessons.

After three years in Wolverhampton it seemed
right to move. We had been actively working to
help find a successor before thinking about our own
move. Then meningitis had intervened. Although a
new challenge was the last thing I wanted right
then, the letter from CPAS did seem part of God's
plan for our future; and we took time out of my

convalescence to visit Sheffield.

Moving

Having begun my ministry in Manchester I thought that at least I knew something about rain! However, Sheffield seemed to need to prove itself the equal of Manchester as far as that was concerned. We saw little of Sheffield on our visit, other than the misted up windows of the car in which we were driven around the city. The striking roof beams of St Thomas's looked like the ideal basis — if the building was turned upside down — for a twentieth-century ark. Even the pub opposite the church was called the Noah's Ark!

The day of my institution as vicar of St Thomas's, Crookes, was to prove wetter still. From early dawn until well after everything was over, it rained and rained. What is more, the size of the raindrops and their force seemed to move up a notch every hour. Our respective families were soaked just making it up the drive. The house was a sea of dripping coats and umbrellas, and every window was steamed up, preventing any viewing of the large garden we had inherited. Each journey, first to the church for the service, then to the nearby Tapton Hall of Residence of Sheffield University for the reception, and then back to the Vicarage, was a mad scramble and a battle against the elements.

I have one abiding memory of the service. It was when the archdeacon takes the new incumbent by the hand and 'sets him in the customary stall'. This necessitated walking down the length of the choir stalls, hand in hand with the archdeacon. Distracted by the emotional and physical awkwardness of the manoeuvre, I failed to negotiate my way around the tall but narrow howitzer shell (one of the least appropriate forms of ecclesiastical furniture) containing a splendid display of flowers. Over they went, saved from total disarray only by a quick hooking movement which my ankle made by way of automatic response.

'For the new vicar of Crookes,' said one of the speakers welcoming me to my first job as an Anglican vicar, 'we looked around the Church of England for the biggest crook we could find: we are delighted to introduce him to you today!' It was meant as a joke, but seemed to sum up the awkwardness of the event and the whole weekend. Though the Sunday services went well enough, the after-church interview, which Ann and I experienced from a panel of people, felt more like a hostile grilling. There was a barbed and suspicious note behind the questions.

It was an unnerving start. I had probably not fully recovered from the meningitis, and was greeted on every side by new situations. Two curates came with the job, but I did not really know what to do with them or how to run a team. I struggled particularly to relate to the church. In Wolverhampton, when new moves were afoot, I had spent time with each of the eight members of the church committee talking ideas through in their homes before anything got as far as the agenda. There was no way that I could do that with a couple of hundred people.

Roots

I was also having to work myself back into the

evangelical world, since most people in the church in Wolverhampton were gloriously unaware of such a term. Indeed one of the leaders in the church in Wolverhampton paid me a fascinating compliment just before I left. He was telling me about a friend of his whose church was unhappy. 'They are having a terrible time,' I was told. 'Mind you,' he added, 'the Vicar is an evangelical or something.' Despite having been led to faith by me, and himself leading others to faith, he had never met this strange breed of Christians. If I had thought more quickly I could have said 'and so are you'.

Not that I was a stranger to that world. My family had come to faith some fifteen years earlier, mainly as a result of the Billy Graham crusades at the end of the 1950s. As a family we had been very occasional church-goers. If we managed both Easter and Christmas services in any one year, we would collapse from religious exhaustion in the next and not be seen for another year. Then my eldest sister came to faith through a Crusader Bible class, and began to pray for the rest of the family. God heard that prayer. Within eighteen months both my parents, my other sister, myself, two aunts, two cousins, and my grandmother (in her eighties) all came to faith. In due course both my sisters married Anglican clergymen, so we became a clergy family.

As a family we were enormously helped by the ministry of Michael Bretell, our local vicar in our home town of Woking. We were grounded in the scriptures through his teaching ministry. Summer house-parties, involvement in the Christian Union at Cambridge, and training at the London College of Divinity, all strengthened that evangelical faith.

Moving to an evangelical church was returning to my roots. The biggest adjustment was coping with the changed response to new ideas. Now I had to be ready for the question, 'is it sound?' Before it had simply been 'will it work?' I had enjoyed the experience in Wolverhampton because of the opportunity to apply the lessons I had learnt over the years. My vision remained unchanged, and has done ever since. I wanted to take the scriptures seriously, to live by them, and to seek to apply their truths to the lives of individuals, and in the life of the church. Doing the truth was all important to me.

St Thomas's had those roots. The church had been built in 1840 and had had a long and honourable evangelical tradition. That had not protected it from the ups and downs that every church goes through, but it had given it a firm foundation, and a congregation which knew the scriptures and had confidence in its message.

Inheritance

Ann and I, with our two young pre-school daughters Elizabeth and Katy — joined six years later by Rachel — were enjoying our new home. After a small 'semi' in Wolverhampton with a kitchen and one living room which had to do as sitting room, play room, counselling room and study, we were basking in the space of our new house, and enjoying the first experience of earning over one thousand pounds a year.

We immediately took to Sheffield, built as it is, like Rome, on seven hills with Crookes on the side of the highest of them. The views from the parish over the Don Valley and the city centre to the south-east, and up the Rivelin Valley towards the Peak District to the north and west, are dramatic. 'Crookes' means corner and it has been a village on the west side of Sheffield since the Doomsday Book. People used to come here for their holidays because of the bracing climate. That was before the seaside resort was invented.

Crookes, which had once been a farming area, had steadily been built on until every square inch seems to be covered. It is less than two miles from the city centre, and is placed mid-way between the more clearly defined inner city and suburban areas. Most of the community live in owner-occupied stone-built terraced houses. One of the first things the PCC did after my arrival was to buy a house for the parish worker, Libby Tuson. After the price was agreed, the estate agent rang up and apologised for 'pushing up the price so much'. He added, 'We would not have done so if we had known that the church was buying it.' The price? £950!

Pensioners make up one third of the population of the parish. When they die, their houses are bought by young couples getting married. Older families with teenage children tend to move out to more spacious accommodation. A graph of the parish population's age would look like a dumbell with many young families at one end, many elderly at the other, and a much smaller number of middle-aged people (and teenage children) joining the two together. In a survey done recently on the whole area, it was established that over half of both the male and female population are not married (being single, divorced or widowed).

My predecessor, Michael Cole, came to a small

but well established congregation, with one hundred and fifty worshippers on Sunday. Many of its members had worshipped in the church most of their lives. However, Michael had arrived straight from working among students as a travelling secretary with the Inter-Varsity Fellowship (now UCCF). Combined with that was a skill in evangelistic preaching. Together these began to have an effect, especially on the evening congregation, which became more consciously geared to young adults in general, and students in particular. Previously very few students came near the church.

Allied to this growth was an emphasis on young families, and on family services in particular. Indeed the Church Pastoral Aid Society order of worship for family services, now very widely used, began its life as a joint CPAS-Michael Cole experiment. It was born in Crookes, having arisen out of a desire to reach the growing number of young families in the community who found little point of contact with the Prayer Book services. Marrying these two styles of worship seemed out of the question so a second morning service had been started, geared to this age group.

When I arrived both the morning services were hovering around or below the one hundred mark. They had clearly served the church well, and enabled it to reach young families, but I quickly began to struggle with what seemed a polarised pattern of worship.

Foolishly, at my first parochial church council meeting, I had said something that many new clergy say — and live to regret — namely, that I would not be seeking to make any changes within the first six months. Rather, I would want to see what was happening and find out how people felt, before introducing any changes should that seem right. By the time of the next meeting I knew things had to change. I stuck my neck out and said, 'The family service is childish, and the Morning Prayer service senile: the sooner the two get together the better!' It was not the best way to win friends and influence people. And yet it worked. I had evidently touched on something that most people were feeling. Within six months the most sensitive area in the life of any church — its worship, style, form, and timing — had all been changed. From harvest festival that year we were together in a 10.30am service, which had Sunday schools running in parallel with it, and a monthly family service on the first Sunday of each month.

As a new broom I had been able to sweep clean only because I was articulating what the church was feeling. Over the years I have come to recognise that that is a vital part of leadership, eighty to ninety per cent of which is expressing the mind of those you are leading. Only ten to twenty percent has to do with leading others into new areas and initiating unwelcomed changes. Those changes, however, are what leaders focus on and churches judge them by.

Cross Winds

Outwardly all seemed well. To my great relief the growth of the church continued after my arrival. But all was not well. I knew I was struggling, though at first I could not put my finger on the reason.

I was finding my first church a considerable

responsibility. A wise elderly clergyman had unnervingly said to me 'You go to your first living to make your mistakes; the trouble with going to somewhere like St Thomas's is that you can't afford to make any.' I felt as if I was running fast up the down escalator, and only just making it. It was during this time that I began to have a series of dreams in which I was driving a car. It was always going downhill in reverse. I was applying the brakes but, however hard I pressed, it would not stop. My night-time journeys backwards were long and never ending.

There were many good things about the church. Yet I found it difficult to see God in all the activity. It seemed as if an observer might say, 'What is happening there is simply the result of a vicar working hard.' I knew there was more to life, yes church life, than that.

My concern focused on two particular areas. I was ordained as a pastor and preacher and in neither area was I finding reality. Members of the church seemed to find me easy enough to get on with, but no one ever came for counsel or help. I was simply not functioning as a pastor. I was even more aware of a hollowness when it came to preaching. I taught from, and expounded, the scriptures week by week. But it did not seem to touch me, or the church. I remember wondering if I dared to abandon preaching for six months to see if it made any difference. Then I realised that if it did not, I would be in difficulty. So I continued.

And I prayed. Not, quite honestly, as a noble discipline. No, this prayer was energised by desperation. I knew, deep within myself, that I needed God in a way that I had not hitherto found him.

Looking Back

I had known joy and reality when, back in the fifties at a Christian boys' camp, I had taken my first step into faith sitting on a tree stump one Easter eve. I remember going to bed that night feeling no different and thinking that it had not worked for me, and then waking on Easter morning and sensing in a profound way the dawning of a new day.

As I looked back two things stood out. First was my hunger for the scriptures. In my new found awareness of the reality of God, I asked the camp officer who had led me to faith to show me some scriptures. They became so alive to me. For half-an-hour we went from verse to verse as 'he opened to me in all the scriptures the things concerning the Christ'. I was having my own Emmaus journey. I asked if we could continue for a further half-hour. He was hesitant. Leaders were well trained not to turn the boys into religious maniacs, but he agreed. So we spent a second, and a third, and a fourth period as I pressed him more and more to continue. Finally he had to come clean and admit it. 'I am sorry', he said, 'but I don't know any more verses!' However, his work was done for he had been instrumental in giving me a hunger for, and love of, the scriptures.

The other mark of my early years as a believer was a desire and ability to share my faith. No doubt there was youthful enthusiasm bound up with it, but I was able to lead others to faith. First at school, and later at university, I had seen the Christian groups I was involved with grow as friends came to know God. I knew the joy of the angels in seeing people find faith and encountering God.

But somehow I had lost these joys on the way.

It had been a long haul to ordination following my call to the ministry a couple of years after my conversion. That call meant staying on an extra year at school to get into university. This was followed by two years of national service. Then came three years at Cambridge, and a further two at theological college. Having then done six years as a curate I had now 'arrived'. The trouble was I was so adjusted to being on the journey that I did not know what to do when I did arrive.

Now at last my life's ambition, that call to full-time service of God in the leadership of the church, had been achieved: and it seemed stillborn. The life had gone out of me.

Dark Night

I caught my first glimpse of God coming to me afresh at a surprising time and in a surprising way. I had been in Crookes for nine months. I was looking forward to Christmas and the possibility of a rest during the holiday period. It was Boxing Day (not usually a spiritual high in my walk with God). It was also a Sunday, and I had decided to preach about the boy Jesus in the Temple. The words, from the Authorised Version, spoke to me with clarity. 'Wist ye not that I must be about my father's business?' the boy Jesus had said to his parents. He seemed surprised that they should ever doubt where he was. I was struck by how aware Jesus was of the Father, by the hunger to learn more about him, and by the confidence Jesus had in his relationship with God. I was humbled to see how clearly his attention was on God — not just the things of God. I never knew what effect the sermon had on the congregation. It was probably not powerful enough to break through the turkey barrier, but it spoke to me with great joy and hope. It was one of the most powerful and effective sermons I had heard. I was preaching to myself, and reaching out after the God and Father of our Lord Jesus Christ.

The clouds did not immediately lift: rather the reverse. At that stage I had not read many of the great spiritual classics, and so I was unaware of the whole idea of 'the dark night of the soul', or what one was supposed to do about it. All I knew was that I needed God to make himself known to me. I had walked too long on the outskirts of his ways.

During the opening months of 1972, I found myself reading Luke chapter eleven, which begins with the teaching of Jesus about prayer. First comes the Lord's prayer, followed by the parable of the importunate neighbour, and then the instruction to 'ask...seek...knock' if you want to find the Father 'giving the Holy Spirit to those who ask him' (Luke 11.9,13). One phrase in that passage stood out with enormous clarity and hope. It was from the parable of the importunate neighbour where the man goes to his neighbour and asks for bread 'because I have nothing to set before them'.

'*Nothing to set before them.*' How perfectly that expressed how I felt. I needed life from God if I was to pass it on to others. I clung to those words as my passport into the presence of God. Because these words were from the teaching of Jesus himself, I knew I could count on him to prove true to his word and answer the prayer of my heart.

What I could not foresee was how he would

choose to answer that prayer, or the means he would use.

A Festival of Light

Around this time a new concern for the moral state of the nation was finding focus in a movement called the Festival of Light. In many cities Christians had come together and had marched on their city centre as a witness to the light of Christ. It was a Christian response to the 'swinging sixties' and the permissive society. It was more 'heart' than 'head', but it had a place, and was the event out of which the Care Trust has now grown.

Several of us, clergy and laity, in Sheffield had decided that we should mount such a march in our city, and called in the national organisers to help us plan the event. A major item at the first committee meeting was to choose the chairman. I was aware of some people looking to me. At that point we stopped for prayer. I relaxed back in my chair and surrendered myself to God feeling honoured to be considered, and yet afraid of being asked. With a deep sigh, I expressed my inner attitude: 'Lord, if you want me to do it I'll be scared of handling an event involving thousands; if you don't want me to do it I'll probably be very disappointed: I yield myself to your will.'

That yielding was important. I was expressing faith by letting go of my plans and hopes and fears, and trusting God enough to allow him to do what he wanted. At the personal level, and in the life of the church, this willingness to relinquish control to the God who is utterly trustworthy has proved to be the foundation of so many steps forward.

What happened next was completely unexpected. Quietly, in my head, I was aware of speaking a language I did not know. Emotionally I felt calm and unexcited, but spiritually I was touching something that was profound, beyond me, and what I can still only describe as 'the music of heaven'. It was certainly a heavenly experience. There was a beauty, a peace, a holy awe, and a deep well of spiritual joy, that drew me in. I did not want it to stop. Not least because I had no way of knowing whether it was something I could ever experience again. At last I dared. Just a little stop, at first, and then I found I could start again.

As I drove home I wondered what I would say to Ann. She had known something of my 'dark night' although I had found it difficult to explain it to her because I did not know what was happening or how to express that searching in the dark. I had first been attracted to Ann, when we met at Lee Abbey, by the depth of her own hunger for God. I recalled she had told me once about having spoken in tongues. My problem was not how she would react but what I should say. For I was sure that whatever else this was it was not speaking in tongues. I had been reared on charismatic horror stories, and I knew all the dangers well. I had not swung from the chandeliers, or rolled in the aisles, and besides, I was 'sound', and had been at a committee meeting.

Why God chose to work this way with me, and why he does with many, I do not know. At one level it is such a silly thing to do, yet its effects were profound. This 'least of the gifts' was going to be a trigger that released much life and blessing and joy in the Lord. Slowly at first, but with increasing certainty, the clouds began to lift and the light of

Christ shone through.

Springtime

The first area of my life to be affected was my own worship of God. Using this gift released a flood of praise. I sang in tongues, spoke in tongues, then found myself expressing words of praise in English which I had not composed. They flooded out of my soul with love for God, and joy in the presence of Jesus. Desperation gave way to delight. Now my praying was warmed by an eagerness for, and a thankfulness to, the one who was making himself a reality to me.

The second change was a freedom to speak of Christ in a way that did not end up in a religious argument but in the passing on of life. I was speaking from experience when I talked to others about knowing God. I could not but speak of the things that I had seen and heard. That summer four very down-to-earth Crookes families came to faith. It happened as a result of baptism visiting. As I had inherited a firm baptismal discipline, and was seeking to continue it in a modified form, they were often difficult sessions. Now I saw God breaking through, giving me not just words but life to communicate.

The third evidence of new life was in my preaching. I began to enjoy it, and look forward to it. I sensed the congregation being challenged by what I said. I now had 'something to set before them'. This found focus in a series of sermons on Joseph. I was astonished to discover just how charismatic he was, with his dreams and visions and words of wisdom and gift of prophecy. However, I was also made aware of a deeper note. I was seeing the Cross at work in him. God took Joseph through a long and hard path to purify his character and his faith. God's love allowed suffering into Joseph's life in order to deal with the pride and other impurities in him. Here was a man in the making in the crucible of God's purposes for him. I was seeing the connection between the Cross and Pentecost.

The fourth change was that people started coming to me seeking counsel.

A fifth sign of new life was that people came to faith while I was away on holiday. Here now was a church where something more than 'a vicar working hard' was taking place.

In the summer of that year of personal renewal I was able, during August, to give further time to prayer. A disturbing thing happened. When I prayed I cried. It kept on happening. Over a three week period I slept, ate, and did a bit of church work, but most of the time I cried. I did not know what I was crying about, I was just crying. For three weeks it continued. It had to do with my relationship with God, my relationship with Ann, and with the whole area of my emotions.

At the heart of this experience there was peace, a sense of cleansing and healing. Only with hindsight did I understand what was going on. God was liberating my emotions. Not that I suddenly became of a different temperament, but I began to be aware in a new way of my feelings, and those of others around me. The emotional picture was changing from black-and-white to colour!

Later I read Simon Tugwell's book *Did You Receive the Spirit?* and found there was a tradition, in the monastic movement, of receiving the Spirit through tears. I had imagined I was the first person to have had this experience. I was not out of my mind after all; rather, I was in good company.

Chapter Two

CHURCH IN THE MELTING POT

A casual observer could be forgiven for thinking that I introduced charismatic renewal into St Thomas's. Certainly I encouraged the faith and expectancy once they emerged, but I was more on the receiving end in the early stages. Struggling to find God afresh in a time of spiritual dryness I was seeking after him myself rather than planning how to take the church anywhere.

In the church, others were coming into the same experience. A sense of excitement and expectancy was abroad. Testimonies were being gossiped around the church about how God was changing people's lives. By the time I surfaced from my wrestling in prayer, I realised that I had fellow-travellers on the road of renewal. That meant one sure thing — problems!

Signs of Life

Our worship was one of the first places where change was evident. Not that the form changed immediately. We still used the Prayer Book services, and had a robed choir. But the whole feel changed. People came with anticipation and excite-

ment expecting to meet with God. A new quality of
reverence and awe was growing at the same time
that love and devotion were being expressed to
God.

A sign of what was happening within the congregation was the impact on those who had newly
come into the church. One such person turned up
one Sunday evening purely of her own accord. She
was hungry for God. She had little or no sense of
sin, only a deep longing for reality in life and in
relationships. She had dropped out of her teaching
career, moved into drug-taking, and dabbled in
eastern religions. In her hunger for meaning she
tried church. Not that she picked a good night. It
was a two-hour Prayer Book communion service
which included a thirty-minute exposition of the
first chapter of the book of the prophet Haggai.
Here was no racy evangelistic service. But there
was worship, and the sense of the presence of God
touched her heart. At the end of the service she was
weeping in the pew. Those who went to comfort her
were surprised by her response. 'I'm so happy, I'm
so happy,' she kept repeating. 'I feel forgiven right
the way through me, it's wonderful.' This young
woman was going to need help in understanding
who had brought her that forgiveness and how she
could rebuild her life on a new basis. But it
happened, and when I last saw her fifteen years
later she was a happily married Christian woman
through whom God was bringing that same forgiveness to others.

A young Christian man who had just moved to
Sheffield knew he needed the support of other
believers. On his first Sunday, not knowing the city,
he set out looking for a church. He walked for

half-an-hour without finding one and was on the verge of giving up when he heard a church bell. It tolled for him. He headed for it through the rain and was drawn into the worship and fellowship, and is still with us fifteen years later.

New life was perhaps most evident in the mid-week fellowship, a prayer meeting of twenty or so people, which had been started by Michael Cole. It was growing as a result of an increasing hunger for God, and was about to move out of the vicarage because we could no longer fit everyone in. A greater openness was evident. Laughter could frequently be heard even in our times of prayer. Joy and enthusiasm were growing. This group was the vital praying heart of the church.

From the start I had said that if this experience was of God it was for us all, and if it was not of God the sooner it went away the better. I was committed to not having a separate charismatic prayer group. It proved an important decision in holding the whole church together. There were tensions even in this prayer meeting because of what was happening, but we were mixed up together, the 'pros', the 'antis', and the 'don't knows'.

Into this situation stepped Jean Darnall, a colourful American Pentecostal pastor, who with her husband, had heard God's call to come to England and help strengthen the movement of the Spirit beyond the bounds of their own denomination. She had been involved in helping us with the Festival of Light march which had drawn four thousand Christians together to march through the city. One Sunday evening Jean preached for us. In a powerful and disarmingly simple way, she told of the joys and pains of seeking to follow God wherever he led. God used her visit to fan the flames of renewal.

However, while these good signs of new life were emerging, there were other reactions too. It was a puzzling time even for those enthusiastic about what was happening. For those who were suspicious, or even hostile, the situation became increasingly tense.

Thunderclouds

The rumblings began at a parochial church council meeting in the summer of 1972. As so often on these occasions, pent-up fears and frustrations surfaced about some minor detail onto which, like a scapegoat, all the anger was attached.

Painful things were said, and harsh accusations made. Deep suspicions were expressed, and we departed in disarray. My instinct in such a situation is not to defend myself. Ann was sure it would have helped if I had sought to defend myself because I had given the impression that I accepted all the accusations. At the heart of what was being said was the fear that I had somehow abandoned the scriptures. The fact was that the scriptures had led me to this experience. I now believed more of them, and saw more of them as relevant for today than I had previously done. Indeed one of the most abiding memories of those days and of the years since is of God taking away the brackets I had put around the scriptures. Less and less have I been able to take up the attitude 'true then — but not to be practised today'.

It soon emerged that those who were against the renewal, though few in number, were among the

most articulate in the church. There were about six
people in all. As the weeks passed by and the
rumblings in the distance got nearer, someone in
the church pointed me to a verse in Isaiah: 'Though
you search for your enemies, you will not find
them' (Isaiah 41.12).

That word was to be fulfilled in a short time with
three of them leaving to join other churches and the
other three staying and accepting the situation.
Both sides showed growing patience and understanding of each other and a commitment to hold
together in unity even when we found it difficult to
be of one mind.

Tense though this time was we did have our
lighter moments. Terry Pratt, a French-speaking
Welshman, later told me of his reaction to what was
happening. At first he was strongly opposed to all
things charismatic, and especially to speaking in
tongues. One Sunday he was in church next to
someone about whom he had dark suspicions. He
was sure this man was singing in tongues under
cover of the hymns. As a determined protest to
such goings-on Terry decided to sing the last hymn
in Welsh. His sense of triumph at drowning out the
singing of his neighbour was short-lived. Immediately after the service ended a lady who was
new to the church and had been sitting behind
Terry came up to him and said 'It was so lovely to
hear you singing in tongues in the last hymn!'

While such tensions existed in the PCC I was
aware that the whole church had seemed to
withdraw emotionally. Instinctively they probably
sensed trouble and stood to one side to avoid
getting hurt themselves.

At that time the Navigator group of Christians at

the university all worshipped at St Thomas's. Only later was I to learn that one of their number had been told by one over-zealous member of the church that unless he spoke in tongues he did not have the Spirit. In those days the group was rather more regimented than now. Today, individuals choose for themselves where to worship, a good number choosing to do so at St Thomas's. However, then, the result of the leader's disquiet was that one Sunday they were all there and the next Sunday fifty regular worshippers had gone. We felt the loss.

Eyesore

We missed the Navigator group for two reasons. First, it drew the attention of the whole church to the 'charismatic disturbances' that until then were really only evident to members of the church council and those who regularly attended the mid-week fellowship. Second, it came at a time when the commitment of the whole church was going to be tested. We were to have the first gift day since I became vicar.

That year the government and local council had mounted a clean-up campaign of cities under the title Operation Eyesore. The church grounds fully fitted the scheme. The small churchyard had well over two hundred tall and totally black headstones. It was surrounded by a six- to seven-foot high wall with the narrowest of gateways — so narrow that coffins had to be posted through it because it was not possible to get a coffin and undertakers through the gate at the same time. A passer-by stopped me one day and asked, 'Do they still hold services in that church?' It was an understandable question.

The only indication that we did was a pathetic sign sticking over the top of this wall saying 'Welcome'. The whole setting said 'Keep out'.

The PCC had decided to take the opportunity of Operation Eyesore to remove some of the head-stones, renew the paths, and in particular to lower the walls and widen the gateway. The government would fund half the cost. Our part was to find £1,250 within six months. The problem was that it looked as if, humanly speaking, it was beyond us. Two hundred and fifty pounds had been the previous highest figure for a gift day. Yet it seemed too good an opportunity to miss.

With the experience of Manchester and Wolverhampton behind me, I launched into the venture with faith and enthusiasm. The PCC were cautious, some expressing doubts about whether it was right to pray specifically — as I had done and encouraged the church to do — for not less than £1,250 on the day. The gift day was just over a month after the Navigator group had left. Although I was confident of God, having faced stiffer challenges to faith in Wolverhampton, I was increasingly uncertain about the readiness and response of the church.

That concern was increased by the evidence of a great sluggishness in prayer. Three evenings of prayer had been planned for the two months leading up to the gift day. Each evening was held in church and divided into half-hour periods. People were encouraged to come and go as they felt able. For the first two evenings we never reached double figures in any half-hour period. It was hardly a boost to faith.

Somehow the *Sheffield Star* got hold of the fact that we were praying for 'Not less than £1,250' on the gift day: so there we were in print.

The Sunday before the gift day I was at a particularly low ebb after the evening service, which felt very much smaller now that the Navigators had gone. The attendance of 112 is printed indelibly on my memory. What made that figure worse was that it was the biggest congregation of the day. I had preached on the subject of giving, having discovered in Manchester that there is no point in preaching on giving on a gift day — by then it is too late for people to respond in prayerful sacrifice. I could see no way that we as a church would be ready to handle the challenge of the target for the next Sunday.

The churchwarden, Ernest Renner, shared my concern and was aware of my despondency. When everyone had left church he took me to the communion rail and poured out his heart in prayer, for me and for the church. It was enormously comforting and supportive.

God in Ernest!

Ernest Renner had lived in Crookes all his life, and had been a choirboy before the war. The church was now very different from the church in which he had grown up. Yet his love for the Lord overcame the patterns of the past. Ernest had been one of the churchwardens responsible for appointing me as vicar. He had not been involved in much of the theological debate going on at the time, but he was quick to discern where God was at work and amazingly ready to be in an unfamiliar place as soon as he sensed that God was wanting him to be there.

After prayer he simply said, 'Remember Gideon,

Robert, and don't worry.' He reminded me how Gideon's army had been so divinely reduced in preparation for the battle ahead, and suggested we were going through a similar process of pruning and preparation.

I went home anxious, yet encouraged.

That Wednesday was the final in our series of evenings of prayer. This time the church turned out in force, with about one hundred members attending for some part of the three hours. The church had obviously got the message about the importance of the forthcoming gift day, and about the vital part that prayer must play.

At the end of the evening Ernest Renner came to tell me about a remarkable dream he had had about St Thomas's the previous night. The church was full of light, full of people, and full of praise to God. It was a wonderful scene. As he looked around he realised that he did not know any of the people. Then the responsible churchwarden obviously surfaced in his dream. He realised that he did not know who the stewards were, or even if there were any: and the collection was about to be taken. He was helpless. Just when this joyful scene was about to turn into a nightmare, Ernest realised that the taking of the collection was almost over. From somewhere among the congregation a silent army of stewards had quietly and efficiently taken it up. As the worship continued Ernest woke to discover it was a dream.

It had been such a wonderful promise of good things to come — not least in the light of our shared gloom of the previous Sunday. Yet, what was he to make of this vast sea of faces, none of whom he knew? It took some while for Ernest to come to peace about that. He realised that the changes taking place might drive all the familiar faces out, though that did not happen. Later he saw it as God's promise of a new generation of St Thomas's people to take over the baton from his own. In due course it was to cause him to stand down as churchwarden because of his fear of standing in the way of this new generation: such was the grace of God in him.

It had clearly been a profound spiritual experience for him and it was not until the early 1980s when we were back in the new St Thomas's that he was willing to tell others about it. Then, out of the blue, he came up to me after one service with glistening eyes full of joy and wonder, saying, 'It has happened, Robert, it has happened.' It took me a while to recall the vision and realise that something in the new setting, the full church, and a whole new generation of stewards, had triggered in him an awareness of just what God had done among us over those years.

The Gift Day

I had said that I would announce the total for the gift day at the end of the evening service. The congregation was larger than the previous week, and a sense of expectancy was in the air — tinged with a few nervous jokes and comments. Clearly not everyone had the gift of faith. One elderly lady in the church shook me by the hand as she left after the evening service and simply said, 'Good night, vicar, I'm not staying to share the disappointment!' It was not sufficient to shake me as I had known that the morning offering had taken us past the one thousand pounds mark. Even I, however, was not prepared for the size of the evening offering. Many had stayed on for the now familiar cup of coffee which we served after the evening services. When the time came to announce the result I teased the congregation a little (something that was to become quite a feature of gift day announcements). 'First, the bad news,' I said. 'We have not got one thousand two hundred and fifty pounds.' I paused. 'What we do have,' I said, ending the suspense, 'is *three* thousand and seventy-four pounds!'

A great cheer went up, followed by an excited buzz of conversation and general rejoicing. I called for order so that we could turn to God in praise and prayer. How it flowed! Joy, thanksgiving, celebration and sheer relief were all mixed together in our praise.

One of the great joys down the years at many such days has been the way in which the whole church's response is one of marvelling at what God has done among us. No one talks about what we have done or achieved or raised. It is, and it feels like, grace — God's giving to us of which we have been privileged to be a part.

More to Come

As well as joy, a sense of awe soon fell on the church as the word got round. This had been a wholly unexpected turn of events. It had never occurred to any of us that we would see the total more than doubled. We did not actually need the extra money. But then the response of the church was not a material or financial one. We felt we were in the presence of God.

It was a master stroke of timing as far as the charismatic tensions were concerned. Here was an event that all could rejoice in, and in which all could see the hand of God.

I decided that we should hold an additional evening of prayer, early in December, to do two things. Obviously we wanted and needed to take time to give thanks to God for what he had done. 'This is the Lord's doing and it is marvellous in our eyes' (Psalm 118.23) summed up how we felt.

Secondly, we seemed to have hit the jackpot. It is not a holy word but it expressed just how we felt. We had evidently done the will of God and been in line with his plans. What might happen if we lined up the whole of the life of the church to his will?

So we returned to God in praise and prayer. Again we followed the three-hour pattern broken up into half-hour periods. This time there was a lot more coming and a lot less going. The majority were there for the whole period. There was enthusiastic and heartfelt praise, and sober prayer and intercession for the church. The impact of the renewal was now filtering through to our way of praying. We no longer needed to fill the gaps between prayers, but rather to enjoy the presence of God in the silence. We were expecting answers there and then to some of the things we prayed about. We were ready to hear what God said.

In the midst of all this a picture came into my mind, and with it a running commentary. It was not a prayer, as it was evidently addressed *to* me not *from* me. Yet it was not anything like a sermon or a talk, not least because it was not my idea. I was listening to what I was saying as though someone else was saying it. Later on I realised that this was a prophecy but, never having heard anything like this before, I had no category into which to put it. Not quite knowing what was happening, I spoke out.

The picture was of the church grounds. My attention was on the fact that the church was less than half built. The tower was completed which enabled me to recognise that I was looking at St Thomas's. All around the site there were stones scattered in an untidy and jumbled manner.

I was seeing the church in the making. It was being built, not experiencing demolition. All this took about half a minute for me to see and grasp. There were no words. As I was surveying the scene a strong urge to speak came on me. As no one else was praying I spoke out. It was a commentary on what I was seeing.

> *'I am building my church in this place. I am not calling you now to gather more stones, for they are all here on the site. But they are scattered and separate. I will build my church with these stones, but for this to happen they must be joined to each other, cemented together in love. As that happens those who are hurt and needy will be drawn to this place. They will find shelter from the storm, and strength and refreshment to go out to serve me in the world. But, remember, those stones must be built together, cemented together in love, if my church is to be built.'*

The only problem we ever had with this prophecy was doing it!

Fellowship

We had heard this word about being cemented together in love, but we did not know how to go

about it. We started by preaching about love. We
looked at what the scriptures had to say about love
and fellowship. We studied all the 'one another'
verses in the New Testament. Six months later we
had the courage to ask ourselves, 'Is the church any
more loving?' It is a dangerous but healthy question
to ask. Though we were not aware of any great
tensions, or personal conflicts, we had to admit that
we could not see any real evidence of the church
being more loving.

At this point two important things happened.
First, David Hughes joined the staff team. I had
known David slightly from my theological college
days. I was now aware that he was looking for a
move. He came up in the late summer of 1972 to
have a preliminary visit. It was going to be a big
step for David, a bachelor, to leave his family and
friends and come north. I was in no doubt that he
was the man I wanted. He was more experienced in
the work of the Holy Spirit, and in the exercise and
discipline of the charismatic gifts, than I was. He
was a fine pastor and preacher, and a man of
prayer. Ann and I took to him immediately.

I found myself praying specifically. 'Lord, if you
want to do a significant work here, I must have
David's help.' That prayer was not only answered,
but proved to be very true. David arrived just after
Easter 1973 and immediately gave help in our
discerning how to act on this from God about
being cemented together in love.

Second, we re-discovered John 5.19 in which
Jesus says, 'The Son does nothing of his own
accord, but only what he sees the Father doing; for
what the Father does, that the Son does also.' It has
been, ever since, a text on which much of the

leadership is based: seeking to discover what God is doing, and then joining in. The cost of doing so is in letting go of our plans; its benefit is the security of being in the will of God.

We began to ask, 'What is the Father doing?' We realised that God was bringing us together in small groups. Several women's Bible study and fellowship groups had started, with Ann and Libby Tuson, the parish worker, and others leading. David had begun a men's group. We began to realise that we had been describing love in terms of mutual care, practical help, and honest openness to one another. Yet it is not possible to practise this at any depth with — as the church was now — over three hundred other people. We needed a manageable sized group in which to practise this love.

Out of this the idea of supporting fellowships arose. We called them this because it expressed the role we had defined for them in the life of the church. They existed to help us to *support one another to be effective for God in the world.*

It seemed an obvious enough title to me, but some clergy had difficulty getting their minds round the idea. One said, 'No wonder you get so much money in your church — with all those supporters' clubs you've started!' Another rang up and said, 'We wonder if you would like to play our church at cricket sometime this summer, we understand you have got a lot of sporters' fellowships in your church.' My explanation must have sounded superspiritual.

It was a venture into the unknown. We decided to do the minimum of organising, but rather to share with the church our vision of such groups in every street of the parish. Our plan was to say to the church: 'If you feel this idea is of God, then go and do something about it, we are not going to organise you.' We did this at the weekend away, at Whirlow Grange, in the spring of 1974. The weekend was a sell-out. At one stage there were ninety of us in a conference centre designed for thirty.

Everyone was enthusiastic. Three months later we stopped to ask ourselves how things were going. There were three groups. Ann and I had started one, David Hughes had started another, and Patrick Coghlan, who had joined the staff in that year straight from college, had begun the third. We were faced with a dilemma. Should we step in and organise groups for the church? It was tempting, but we decided to give it at least another month, and in the meanwhile to pray that others would act. Some had caught the vision, but were having difficulty coping with a church situation where they were allowed to take the initiative. The message needed time to sink in. Within the next month three more groups were started by lay members of the church.

Very soon we were being asked to train the group leaders. We did get them together regularly and we shared with each other what we were learning. But at that stage we refused requests for training on the simple grounds that we knew no more than anyone else. We were starting from scratch, and depending on God to lead us.

Shake Down

The next three years were times of discovering how to enable these groups to function effectively. They were the focus of all our life together. We retained the mid-week fellowship which was the heart of the church and the source of our unity and vision. It enabled the different groups to come together and feel part of the whole.

The consequence of investing so much manpower in these groups meant that they flourished, and were fifteen in number three years later. It also meant that other activities declined. As I saw this I came to the conclusion that fellowship was where God was calling us to put our energies, and that any purely human effort to keep a series of traditional activities going was not right. Without actively trying to stop anything, I found that by not rushing round madly trying to fill every gap which emerged, a series of things ceased.

Lifestyle

What emerged from the launching of supporting fellowships was to have a profound effect on the whole lifestyle of the church. Because we had set them up on a purely geographical basis, people were able to express practical help towards each other. A network of loving relationships was laid down in several areas of the parish through which, in due course, others were drawn to faith in Christ.

We also often managed to break out of the meetings mentality, and drew a clear distinction between *going* to a supporting fellowship (which you could do in a couple of hours a week) and *being* a supporting fellowship, which involves a seven days a week commitment to love our brothers and sisters in Christ.

Coming as they did on the heels of conflict about

the charismatic dimension to the Christian life, the groups had a healing effect. We knew each other by name, not by labels, and learned to live together across the doctrinal, emotional, and social barriers that so often divide.

The fact that we met with those who lived nearest to us often meant that we were meeting with people with whom the only common ground was our mutual commitment to Jesus as Lord.

The level of love and sacrificial care was sometimes breathtaking. One woman who had just been divorced and become alcoholic, with a prognosis of less than six months to live, was cared for, and sacrificed for endlessly. She came to her senses, found faith, and healing, and is alive and well today.

Another couple took a pregnant Christian girl into their heart and home. They helped her through the pregnancy and to break free from a love for the father which was not reciprocated. They, the girl and the whole group, moved on to cope with the subsequent cot death of the child which took place during a supporting fellowship meeting.

Another couple had the gable end of their house declared unsafe weeks before the birth of their first child. It was an end of terrace house so taking down the wall would leave every room exposed to the elements. Their insurance did not cover this eventuality. Within days a bachelor had moved out of his house so that the couple could live there, and enough money had been pledged to cover the cost of the repairs.

Others in great need were taken in, and loved into life. Not that every group flourished all the time, or always had success in its caring, but many did, and the impact on the church was profound. No longer were we separate individuals keeping up a good appearance as we went to church each week. We began to be real as people, to admit our feelings, our doubts, frustrations, and fears: and to love each other through them.

It was costly, but it was also fun. People enjoyed themselves enormously. Many groups went on holiday together, including one with members aged nine to ninety, which went to Scotland for a fortnight. Social events became important as people relaxed. Non-Christian partners of church members joined in: some were won to faith in this way.

Life

Although the development of supporting fellowships was the major emphasis of these years (1973-75), the impact of renewal was spreading much wider.

We were continuously seeing people come to faith, usually through the changed lives of church members. Patrick Coghlan played a particularly vital part in this. He not only won many to faith, but raised the confidence of the whole church to witness to our faith. A survey at the end of this period established that as many as sixty per cent of all those who became believers through St Thomas's attributed the fact to the witness of a friend in the church. No other factor scored as much as ten per cent. This resulted in the steady but undramatic growth of the church. By the end of 1975 the usual Sunday attendance had risen to close on four hundred.

David Hughes was instrumental in introducing worship into the mid-week fellowship, which by 1975 was drawing ninety people each week. With the use of a small worship group our ability to express our praise and to sense the presence of God was steadily maturing. This was carried over into our Sunday services. The gifts of the Spirit were exercised from time to time in the services, but the predominant note was one of the reality of God encountered as much in the sensitive handling of the liturgy, as in any dramatic expression of the charismatic gifts. The newer forms of service were embraced, and some of the older practices, such as chanting of psalms, allowed to lapse. They seemed to be inappropriate hurdles to put in the way of the growing number of newcomers.

Healings happened among us, and prayer for healing became a regular part of our worship pattern. Once a month after both the morning and evening services, we held a shortened form of communion. In this quieter context we introduced prayer for healing. God graciously worked in the lives of a number of people in these services; though just as frequently those who were in need went to their fellowship groups when they needed prayer.

One of the most important consequences of what was happening was that we were coming to terms with ourselves, and so were able to relate in a more honest, open, and understanding way, to each other. God was dealing with deep seated sins and hurts and emotional blockages. Here again David Hughes's skills in prayer counselling was of crucial importance. In addition the supporting fellowships gave us the context in which to be real with one another, rather than to keep up a good image. Out of this a counselling style was developed, which sought to integrate the moral teachings of scripture, some of the insights of modern psychology, and the power of the Holy Spirit to transform the inner person through prayer. Because we were all helping each other in this process it affected the whole way we related to one another.

The influx of new people was having a definite, but subtle and largely hidden, effect on the whole way we operated as a church. Our stewarding of services was becoming more organised, as was the whole life of the church. Two new churchwardens, Eric France and Richard Laughlin, were typical of a new generation emerging in leadership.

A further consequence of all this upheaval within us as people, and within the church, was that we were finding our buildings an increasing problem. There was a growing desire to serve those beyond the bounds of the church. However, there was little that could be done in the buildings we had. They were causing problems too as they became increasingly unsuitable for the new expressions of worship and fellowship. Moreover we were finding ourselves short of space at our bigger services.

Chapter Three

FACING WEST

When I was invited to become vicar of St Thomas's a building project seemed an imminent possibility. By the time I arrived, and to my great relief, the closure of the next door church school (on which the whole plan depended) had been withdrawn and the project shelved. However, by the end of 1975, there were clear indications that God was putting the whole matter back on the church's agenda.

The need was becoming increasingly evident. Our worship had steadily changed its style and form. The existing lay-out became more and more unsuitable. Fixed pews hardly expressed a new found liberty in our relationships. The disused choir stalls pointed to a previous way of leading worship and added to the sense of distance between the communion table and the congregation at just the time that the sacrament was becoming a more vital part of our drawing close to God. The narrow chancel made administration of communion increasingly lengthy as only eight people at a time could kneel at the rail. Our growth as a church was beginning to press the capacity of the building to its limits. Indeed in 1975 we had to turn twenty people away from the carol service because all the standing room in church was taken, and there was nowhere else to put people.

We had made some changes but they hardly fitted with the building as it was. An overhead projector screen now hung next to the pulpit, and was used both for worship songs, and for sermon illustrations. We built a temporary stage at the foot of the chancel steps, and used it for dance and drama, and for the worship team which was playing an increasing part in leading worship. We also brought another table onto this staging and used it for communion. Coffee was now served in the aisles after services though the fixed pews made for very cramped conditions.

Our service to the community was seriously hampered by the lack of anywhere suitable to hold activities.

We were using three buildings, none of which was satisfactory. The church itself was closed for six days a week, and whatever we did, it was always cold in winter. The unisex toilet facilities were an embarrassment. The church hall, a prefabricated building put up in 1964 just as Michael Cole arrived, was out of the way, too small, and a building that defied improvement. We made considerable use of the church school, situated as it was between the church and the main road. We used it for Sunday schools, and for our mid-week fellowship. However, the rental fees were continually being increased so we were discovering just how costly prayer can be! The use of the school buildings was often uncertain because of the stop-start situation of arrangements for letting which reflected varying government decisions about saving money. We were not, of course, allowed to

make any changes to the rooms we did use, so there
was nothing we could do to make them more
appropriate for our use.

It was an untidy, and inefficient, situation.
Clearly the time to act was fast approaching.

An Idea!

The spark that set the whole venture off was the
offer of £25,000 from a housing association to
purchase the land on which our church hall stood.

A solicitor member of the church, through whom
the offer had been communicated, met the two
churchwardens, Eric France and Richard Laughlin,
and myself. It was intended to be a short briefing
meeting: it proved to be a moment of conception.
Richard Laughlin said, with some frustration,
'Can't we do anything with that great barn of a
place which we only use one day a week?' We
began to consider how we could make use of it. As I
talked it over in our kitchen after the meeting, Ann
said, 'Why not move the hall across to the church
site and connect it to the church?'

As soon as I could, I went over and paced it out
— it fitted. However, at the staff meeting the next
day it was dismissed within five minutes as a crazy
idea. The meeting passed on to more sensible items
on its agenda.

But the idea persisted, and over the next few
weeks, Eric and Richard and I began to sharpen up
the ideas and to see the possibilities of moving all
our buildings onto one site by wrapping a new
building around the church. Out of this emerged a
definition of what we were looking for: *an integrated, multi-purpose, flexible-use, maintenance-*

free building.

An *integrated building* was very important to us as an expression of the renewal we had experienced. That renewal had affected the whole of our living. What before had been kept in separate compartments (worship, personal relationships, emotions, life in the neighbourhood) were being integrated around our relationship with God. It was as if the tide of the Spirit had swept in and raised the water level above the separate compartments of our lives, so that all life was one — centred on Jesus as Lord. Worship is not separate from the rest of life but the inspiration for it all. Christian service and worship are two sides of the same coin. We wanted our building to express that. In due course we made sure that the worship area was central, and that everyone coming to the building, for whatever purpose, would see it. We did this both by building the extension around the worship area, and by putting windows into the screen at the back of the area. This meant that everyone who came into the building, whether for Keep Fit, to vote at an election, or for worship would see what was the heart and inspiration of the church's life.

By *multi-purpose* we meant a place where the whole of the life of the church could be expressed. So we needed a games hall and lounge, a kitchen and offices. Moreover, we wanted every area to be flexible in its use and not tied to one form of activity. We resisted labelling rooms in such a way that any group felt that they owned it (like choir vestry, or youth hall). Moreover even the worship area was to be such that it could be used for such things as concerts or social events. This related to the *flexible use* too, expressed in the fact that all the holy furniture (pulpit, communion table, clergy prayer desks) were to be movable, together with the seating for the congregation, so that the worship area was not locked in to one use only.

Our concern about the building being *maintenance free* was that we wanted it to be a blessing to the next generation of worshippers, not a burden. Aware of how often Victorian church buildings have become an obstacle rather than an aid to the mision of the church today, we thought long and hard about how to avoid giving the next generation a problem because of what we had done. Eventually we came to the conclusion that there was no way we could predict the needs of the church in fifty years' time. There were things we could do, however, that would be best designed to help. We prayed quite specifically that what we did do would be led by God to help those who would follow.

When the plans were complete we actually took time to consider how the building could be used if the congregation grew to two thousand, or shrank to fifty, and were confident it could be adapted to meet both eventualities. It was with the next generation in mind that we sought at every point, particularly through the use of brick and timber finishes, to ease the maintenance problems. It was with them in mind that we made decisions, for example, about window frames. Obviously timber window frames would outlast all of us involved in the project, but for long-term cost-effectiveness metal ones were best. We decided to pay twelve thousand pounds for the metal ones, rather than the four thousand pounds which the timber ones would have cost.

Listening

Once the idea of moving everything onto the one
site was grasped we began to share that with the
PCC. By Easter of 1976 it was in full agreement.

It was not my idea but, after the PCC had
decided in principle on the project, it was proposed
that we took time to consult the whole church. It
meant an initial delay of four months; but it
resulted in a large part of the church's membership
being behind the work. We arranged a series of
talkback sessions after both services in June of that
year at which we told the church what we were
thinking, and invited their response. The church
was thoughtful, pressing us with many perceptive
questions; as well as positive, encouraging us in the
direction we were going. On more than one
occasion the church challenged the leaders to faith
— rather than the other way round. And so we
agreed in principle to such a venture in June 1976.
Little did we then realise how hard the way ahead
would be.

Another Gift Day

We decided to hold a gift day that autumn to launch
the work, having not had one since Operation
Eyesore for the re-ordering of the churchyard in
1972. We had briefed the church architect to draw
up some plans which we intended to show to the
church on the gift day. They arrived on the Sunday
before, and the church council saw them the next
day. They were not what we wanted, and at the
talkback sessions on the gift day we had to inform
the church that we had no plans, and had dismissed

the architect. This was not the start we were looking for but we were sure it was the best and, in the long run, the quickest way to proceed.

On the day, £6,670 was given. It was more than double the 'jackpot' figure of 1972 and gave us enormous encouragement that we were indeed on the right path.

In reading that figure, and the ones that follow, it is important to keep them in perspective. There were about two hundred people actively involved in the project, with probably fewer than one hundred and fifty wage earners. A comprehensive and independent survey in 1978 established that forty per cent of the church were earning £1,500 or less (students, and pensioners etc), with a further forty-six per cent earning less than the national average wage, which at that time was £4,000. It was this group of people who, in the course of the next four years, were to give nearly half a million pounds.

Inevitably we had those who said that 'this money should have been given to the poor', or rather 'spent on missionary work'. My answer to this was that if this project was not missionary work we should not be doing it. All Christian giving is missionary giving. Yes, we do need to watch for a proper balance in giving to God's work here, and to the church overseas, but it is all part of the same venture.

Our earlier gift day in 1972, to re-order the churchyard, had resulted in a sustained increase in giving — including to missionary work — and I had no doubt that the same would happen again. Despite the massive financial demands on us as a church our missionary giving continued to climb slowly (from £9,000 a year three years before the project finished, to £12,000 in its final year). Thereafter it rose rapidly, reaching over £50,000 a year within a further three years.

Plans

In January 1977, having interviewed several men, we appointed Robert Potter as our architect. Based in Southampton he was not the most obvious choice. However, he had been involved in two very similar ventures at Millmead Baptist church in Guildford, and at All Souls', Langham Place, London, where Michael Baughen had moved in the early 1970s. We chose him because we judged him to be God's man for the work, and so he proved to be. He continually pushed us to go for the highest standards in materials and workmanship. We have lived to be grateful for, and benefit from, that pressure.

Our first lunchtime meeting with Robert Potter was to prove an enjoyable, entertaining, and creative time. As we outlined our needs we began to talk about how our accommodation problems could be solved. As we were having difficulty describing the buildings we used various items of cutlery to illustrate alternative plans. A tall pepper pot was a great help in representing the tower, which was about the only fixed point in our fluid plans. At the crucial moment a waiter came to serve the next course and removed the pepper pot. We wondered if this was a word from Above!

It emerged that the four of us each had a different way of solving the problem.

At that stage Robert Potter thought we could leave the worship area facing east. My idea was to focus it on the south wall. Richard thought that a north-facing church would give us the most room. It was Eric who argued for turning everything to face west. At least we had covered all the options. It soon became clear that Eric's plan was the only way in which we could add significantly to the building. By demolishing the chancel and vestries and turning the whole building around inside to face the other way a large extension (one hundred feet by forty feet) could be added to what would then be the back of the church. This would be sufficient to contain an entrance area, parish office, and toilets in one third. A further third would be taken up with a games hall, and the final third would be on two storeys and contain a lounge and kitchen at ground floor level, and a balcony to the worship area above it.

To those who were anxious about worship not facing east, I pointed out that 'we are still facing east — it is just that it is the long way round!' In addition to this new work we also planned to renovate completely the existing building, putting in a new heating system, re-wiring, re-laying the floor and carpeting most of the building. We were also going to replace the pews with chairs, and replace all the 'holy furniture'.[1]

Church Extension Project

During this period we decided on the title for the whole venture. We would call it the *Church Extension Project*.

[1] See appendix for plans of the re-ordering of the building.

There was an intended double meaning to this. The most obvious meaning was that we would be extending the church building. The other meaning, however, was important to us. We were aware of a wider calling of God to us to be stretched and extended by reaching out into the local community with the good news and compassionate service of the gospel. The work on the building was not to be an end in itself, but rather the means to the end of making Christ known in the community. The completion of the building project would signal the start, not the finish, of something important.

In order to reinforce this double meaning we also took on the goal of 'doubling the number of believers in Crookes within the next five years (from the start of the project)'. As things turned out we found that we could not handle both at the same time, and it has only been in the second half of the eighties that that greater goal of the extension project has had time and space and energy to become our first priority.

One of the important reasons for setting the work on the building in the wider context of mission was that we needed to see the completion of the work as the beginning of something. When a new supermarket is put up the owners do not then just sit back and enjoy it, rather they know that they are now open for business. By the grace of God we were able to develop that same mentality. The building project was for the kingdom of God — not for the building.

Helping Hands

The whole operation was extremely demanding of

time, and physical and emotional energy. Without the tremendous support, and sharing of the pastoral load, by David Hughes, neither I nor the church could have survived.

The project was run by myself and the two churchwardens, Eric France and Richard Laughlin, who were entrusted by the church council with full authority to manage the whole venture. It was a very high level of trust, and a very effective means of operating. Decisions could be made speedily. Although we were continually reporting back at the earliest moment, we were free to act as we judged best.

Richard and Eric were remarkably suited to this work. Their skills were such that we were aware of God's hand on the project before we had seen it coming. They had been elected as wardens back in 1974 when there was no idea of a building project. They were chosen simply because they were two mature, faith-filled, men who had the respect and confidence of the church. Yet Richard was a qualified chartered accountant, lecturing in accounting and financial management at the university; and Eric was a lecturer in building construction at a college of further education. Someone seemed to know what skills we were going to need.

It was a privilege to work with them, and a special time in the lives of each of us. It was also very hard work with frequent meetings often ending well past midnight. Ann also played a valuable part, not least on the furnishings and fabric side, and was herself, with two others, spending one evening a week for a whole year making the banner which forms the focal point of the worship area. The team was enlarged in the

second half of the project by the addition of
Jonathan Palmer, an architect within the church,
whose professional skill and thoroughness proved
invaluable in dealing with the mass of details and
decisions we constantly faced. Time and time again,
I found myself saying, 'They never taught me that
at theological college.'

The work was very demanding of time and
thought and emotional energy, but it was not
without its lighter moments. One such occasion
sticks in my memory. It was at one of our monthly
meetings with Robert Potter. It was well past
midnight and there was a long agenda still to be
tackled. We decided to take a short break and
naturally fell into conversation with those sitting
next to us. As so often happens it was one of the
other conversations that grabbed my attention. In
the conversation between Robert Potter and Eric
France I thought I heard one of them say 'It's like
the kissing on London commons'! That was not the
sort of conversation I had expected them to be
having. Intrigued, I asked them to repeat what they
had said. Apart from 'kiss marks', rather than
'kissing', I had heard them correctly. With much
amusement they went on to explain to me (a
layman in the building trade) that London commons are the cheapest mass produced brick. Their
appearance is unattractive but they are readily
identified by the 'kiss marks' produced during the
kilning process resulting from the way they are
stacked. They were wanting to avoid such bricks.
My thoughts about the subject of their conversation
had been very different!

Although we worked with the small team we
were continually bringing in other people with

expert knowledge in different areas to help us on specific issues, from how to equip the kitchen to what brief to give the architect about the design of the communion table.

The church council was consistently supportive, and on several occasions stopped to lay hands on us, pray for us, and prophesy over us. It was a great strength to us to know that others knew the strains and were right with us in the work.

Launching the CEP Fund

The gift day in November 1976 had been a one-off event. By the autumn of 1977 we were ready to launch the CEP (Church Extension Project) Fund on a regular basis, calling people not only to give a lump sum on the day, but also to pledge the level of their giving to the project during the next year. This was *in addition* to the regular pledges of giving both to St Thomas's and to missionary work. Now there were three commitments to make.

The gift day in 1977 also saw another first in what was to become a familiar pattern. Our insurance firm required us to have a police escort to the night safe deposit. From then onwards at each gift day we would have police in attendance. That Sunday they escorted £16,170 to the bank. For some reason the media got hold of the details. By the time of the staff meeting on the following morning I had both ITV and BBC camera crews lined up for interviews for their regional programmes, and had been contacted by five national newspapers and a national news agency.

Such was the level of giving that we were calling people to that we did not encourage the usual form of covenanting. Under that form a person pledges a certain level of giving over a seven-year (later reduced by government legislation to a four-year) period. Rather, we encouraged people to give all they could, and then to take out a lump sum covenant which would enable the church to claim back the tax on their giving over the next seven (and later, four) years. This would eventually have the effect of increasing the giving over the whole period by over one hundred thousand pounds.

Prayer

Not only was the vital role of every member seen in the area of giving, it was also evident in the equally important work of prayer. The whole project was surrounded by prayer. We prayed in all our services, and in our fellowship groups. We produced a project prayer, encouraged the church family to use it in their own prayers, and used it regularly in the Sunday services. It read as follows:

Our Father God,

We praise you for calling us to be part of a renewed St Thomas's.

We ask that you will prosper the financing and building of the new church centre.

Make us a renewed people who welcome Christ's ordering of our lives and are empowered by his Spirit for fruitful service.

Take us and use us that the life of Jesus

*our Lord may touch and transform the life
of this community and city and the world
in which you have placed us.*

*We ask this in the mighty name of Jesus our Lord.
Amen.*

We held special evenings of prayer, and days of
prayer. In the final three months we held a weekly
prayer meeting, which resulted in a noticeable
improvement in the building progress. They were
all vital times of meeting with God, hearing his call
to us about our giving, and ways in which we saw
his answers to practical needs such as fine weather
to get the roof on (in February!), and to get the
stone out of the quarry. The latter, as someone
pointed out to me, needed faith to move a
mountain!

Outside Help

Early on in the project we had to decide what we
would do about seeking help from others. Our first
commitment was for us to be giving sacrificially.
We did nothing in the way of approaching others
until that was well under way. We did write to some
former members of the church and received some
help from them. Well on into the project we came
to the conviction that, if we gave all that was
pleasing to God, he was well able to make up any
shortfall by his overruling.

In this attitude we set up a small team to research
the whole area of trust funds. We discovered a
number of such funds which were committed to

giving help to the sort of work we were involved in:
not least a number of evangelical funds. The work
was thoroughly, and prayerfully, done and hundreds of letters were sent out. The great majority
made no contribution. A few, including the Church
Burgesses in Sheffield, and (Methodist) Rank
Foundation, gave between them fifty thousand
pounds, and also helped with interest-free loans of
a further forty thousand pounds. Taking up loans
did not break our principle of opening free of debt,
because we knew that tax-rebate income on money
already given would be forthcoming for several
years after the project ended.

Prayer, personal relationships with trust fund
members, and the providence of God all played
their part in our finally receiving close on sixty
thousand pounds from such sources. Wonderful
though this help was, it was always seen as a
supplement to, not a substitute for. our giving.
Indeed we were told on a number of occasions that
grants had been made specifically because of the
church's own giving.

We also received advice, encouragement, and
great support from Michael Baughen, who by that
time had led All Souls' Church, Langham Place,
London, through a major building project. In
thankfulness to God for his blessing on their project
five years earlier, All Souls' held a gift day for the
needs of other such faith-ventures. As a result of
that, and individual gifts from members of that
church, we received around twelve thousand
pounds. The money itself was enormously valuable,
but we valued even more highly the sense of others
cheering us on.

There was an interesting sequel to that gift.

Several years after our project was completed we held a 'faith building projects' gift day, to help two churches which had their own half-a-million-pound projects. Although very few St Thomas's people knew much of the other situations, over ten thousand pounds was given. A year later I heard that one of those churches had had a similar thanksgiving gift day at which sixteen thousand pounds was given for another church they were involved with. Generosity is catching!

Chapter Four

THE LAST STONE

Nearly two years were to pass, after the launching of the CEP Fund in November 1977, before any building work began. Progress seemed very slow. Back in 1976, one year after we had had the initial idea, I spoke of the need to be patient because the whole work might not be completed until 1978. We would need to wait two years. When 1978 came we were still two years away. We never seemed to get any nearer the starting date for building. It felt as if we were running up the down escalator.

If that was true about the timing, how much more so was it true of the costs. Everything seemed to work against us. We were building in the time of the highest inflation this country had probably ever known. At times it was running at over twenty per cent. Every delay cost money.

The gift day in 1978 reached just twelve thousand pounds and showed the struggle we were having to maintain the momentum of faith and hope and sacrifice. It was not easy to know whether to rejoice in this further step forward in giving, or to be disappointed that it was considerably less than the previous year. I found myself comforting the church that 'only twelve thousand pounds' had been given.

When we first launched the project we talked about needing a quarter of a million pounds. However, we had not made allowance for furnishings and equipment, so our real starting costs were actually £300,000. By 1978 that had increased to £400,000. When we actually accepted the lowest tender we knew we were well over the £500,000 mark, and in the final issue — eighteen months after starting the building work — the cost worked out at £633,000!

Since my school days I had frequently had migraine, during which my sight started to swirl around. Beginning at the outsides of my vision the blurring moved into the centre until I could see practically nothing. One of the effects of my experience of the Holy Spirit in 1972 was that these migraines were a thing of the past. I was to have one more: it came on in a moment. I had just collected Robert Potter from the station. On the ten minute journey home he told me we needed to be thinking in terms of £400,000. My sight just lasted out long enough to complete the drive. I immediately retired to bed and left Eric and Richard to handle the meeting.

Although time seemed to stand still, we certainly did not. There was much hidden work to be done. Plans had to be worked out and the church consulted about the size of the whole venture. Planning permission from the town council, and faculty authority from the diocese, had to be obtained. It took many hours of meetings: or rather, hours of waiting outside meetings, before our way was clear. The town council insisted that the whole of the new work should be done in stone, which added a further sixty thousand pounds to the costs. We also had to attempt to placate some conservation groups. Contractors had to be considered, short-listed, and decided upon.

Holding on

We had determined to walk by faith in this project, though little did we realise, as we set out with much enthusiasm, just how hard the way would be.

The 1979 gift day typified our experience.

On the Sunday before the gift day Michael Baughen had come from London to preach for us on the subject of giving, not least out of the experience of All Souls' (recorded in Mary Endersbee's book *Miracles at All Souls*). His sermon was an enormous boost to the faith of the church. He obviously knew exactly what we were going through, spoke from the heart, and built faith in God into the whole church. The impact of the sermon was evident the next Sunday when we were able to rejoice that £25,000 had been given in one day. That did not include pledges for the coming year or anticipated tax rebates, but simply the amount of cash and cheques given by the five hundred worshippers that day. That was followed by a surge of giving in the next three weeks which meant that within a month we were £40,000 nearer our target.

Then came the bombshell.

On the Monday of Christmas week we had a letter from the quantity surveyor telling us that in view of the fact that inflation in the building industry was by now running at over twenty-five per cent he thought it would be prudent to allow an extra £40,000 on the costs. All the deeply sacrificial giving of the past month had been wiped out at a stroke. To replace that would involve us in giving to the hilt and beyond. This seesaw of hope and despair were all part of the experience.

As a result of these escalating costs we never seemed to move any nearer the target. In the autumn of 1976 we needed £300,000. By the summer of 1980, with only six months to go, we had already given more than that, and yet we still needed £300,000.

Perhaps we had imagined that faith is some wonderful feeling of elation, akin to floating on cloud nine. We discovered that it is the God-given ability to keep going and keep holding on when everything around is going wrong and points to failure. It is the opposite of sight. It is also the friend of despair. As we came back to the scriptures we saw how great prayers of faith were so often the fruit of despair: Hannah weeping before the Lord about her childlessness; Hezekiah crying out to God after he had been told by the prophet to put his house in order because he was about to die; Daniel and his friends seeking the interpretation of Nebuchadnezzar's dream as they waited for their execution along with all the other wise men for failing to either know the dream or its interpretation. The lepers, and people like blind Bartimaeus, who came to Jesus, were driven by despair. That we found was the seed-bed, not the enemy, of faith. God is met more often at the breaking point than on the crest of the wave.

We also took heart from the experience of Abraham. Though he knew that the promise of a child had been given to him by God, his faith often wavered. Sometimes he tried to answer the prayer in his own way and energies, and sinned. His faith was not perfect, or always present. It was God's faith, his faithfulness to Abraham, that sustained him. So with us there were times when few if any held on by faith. It was then that we knew God was holding on to us. In the painful process we were breaking free of Western man's need to make faith something that we do and achieve. We were finding it to be a God-given response to his faithfulness in the midst of adverse circumstances.

Sacrifices

The magnitude of the project meant that it was dependent upon the faith and sacrifice of the whole church family. That was incredibly forthcoming. The high level of giving was evidenced in many stories.

One couple gave the deposit on their house and delayed their wedding until they had re-saved the deposit. Some went without holidays, many put off replacing cars and furniture in order to give. Several couples who were both earning gave the whole of one salary to the building project. One other sacrifice that we did not discover until nine months or so after the completion of the project was the extent to which young couples had delayed having a family. Within a year of the opening there were twenty-two births in the church family!

Making a Start

In January 1979 we moved out of St Thomas's and took up residence in the nearby Baptist church where we worshipped for ninety-nine Sundays until our return. In June the contractors moved in, and the faith of the past four years was rewarded with sight. For the first time there was concrete evidence of the vision we had had in our minds for so long.

The church and the local community reacted in very different ways to the building work. The church saw this move as enormously encouraging, and a spur to faith and giving. The giving escalated throughout this period. Indeed in the final year the CEP element of the Sunday collections rarely fell below £2,000 a Sunday, even during holiday months. 'Here,' the church felt, 'is what we have been working and waiting, praying and giving, for.'

While the church had been sustained by faith, it was quickly evident that the community was dependent on sight alone. Initially sight spoke only of demolition and disturbance, and the negative and hostile reactions were considerable. It was during this period that I had a letter addressed to 'The Vandal of Crookes'. However when, in due course, the new parts of the building started to go up the mood in the community rapidly became positive. Well over one thousand people from the community came to inspect the buildings in the first week when we opened the church to the public each night.

By early 1980 the new work was beginning to rise from the ground.

On to Completion

The whole church was kept as fully in the picture as we knew how. We were not only regularly holding prayer meetings, but were also providing fact sheets which kept people up to date with the situation. In the last eighteen months we held quarterly gift days, and on them we had talkback sessions at which we kept everyone informed. During the final year we also arranged to have site visits on three occasions. After the morning service we processed over to the church, sang and prayed, and saw what progress was being made.

Although we had to delay the opening by three months, it was a year of mounting excitement and enthusiasm. At last we began to need less than £300,000. Yet there still seemed to be a vast distance to go. When we returned home from our summer holidays early in September 1980 the target was down to 'only' £200,000. The problem was that there were only one hundred days to go.

It seemed impossible, though I was often quoting Hudson Taylor who once said, 'There are three stages in a work of God: impossible — difficult — and done.' By this time I was wanting to add two qualifications to that saying of his. First, I reckoned that there are three stages of impossibility that a work of God goes through: impossible — more impossible — and most impossible. Second, we discovered that the impossible stage for us laster four years, the difficult stage four days, and then it was done in a moment!

By the time we reached the final gift day in November 1980 (three weeks before we were due to open) the target had come down to £54,000.

My abiding memory of that gift day was the difficulty I had in announcing the target. After the service, as a packed church waited to hear the result of the day, praise spontaneously erupted from the congregation and was picked up by the worship team. Song after song was sung. Several times I stood up, only to be 'worshipped down'! God, not giving, was the focus of our faith. I, and the police escort, had to wait twenty minutes before I was able to tell the church what the financial situation was as a result of the giving that day.

An incredible £39,000 had been given. So much had been covenanted that we were assured of a further £11,000 of tax rebates over the next four years: this was all covered by the interest-free loans we had received. We had advanced fifty thousand pounds in one day and were now within four thousand pounds of our target. The giving continued in the final three weeks so that, when, three days before the opening service, I received a cheque for £1,500 our target had been reached. God had shown his faithfulness to us.

For the sake of accuracy I need to complete that picture, which proved to be rather more complex than we had first realised. It became clear in the last six months of the project that we were receiving bills well over six months after the work to which they related had been completed. However, it was not until we had them that we knew how accurate the estimates had been. We realised that when we opened the building we would not actually know what the cost was, or whether we had achieved the required total. In the last few months we decided to leave the total cost figure, which we communicated to the church, unchanged. The church council agreed to go for that target, and to close down the fund and make no more appeals once the building was re-opened, until the final figure was known. If, when the final bill was in, there was a shortfall then we would be more than ready to trust that a final gift day would be accepted gladly by the church family to complete the whole work.

The final bill did not arrive until two years later, in early 1983. The implication was that we needed a further £25,000. So, in June 1983, we held a Finishing the Task gift day, and saw over £27,000 given on the day. The task was completed.

Saturday, December 13, 1980

The final week was frantic indeed. On the Wednesday the wardens came to me and said they could see no way in which the building could be ready for the opening service on the Saturday. I could see that there was no way we could do anything but have the service then, though the inside of the church looked about a month off completion to the eye of an amateur.

A great army of people rallied round, some such as Jonathan Palmer working through the night to get the church ready. When the bishop came for a rehearsal on the afternoon of the opening service I had to say, 'In the service, bishop, we would like you to sit here, but whatever happens don't sit there now because the paint is still wet!'

Practically no one had seen the church ready before the actual service. Even for myself, feeling as if I had lived in the building for the past months, the sight of the completed work was breathtaking. The whiteness of the walls, and brightness of the lights (including eight theatre spotlights mounted on the roof beams) made the church brilliant. The response of the church family as they came in, and especially as they saw the banner set in the centre archway of the worship area, was one of stunned awe. A number were in tears of elation and thankfulness to God.

At one of our most discouraging times in the project Eric France had brought to us a text from Zechariah which we printed on the order of service. It summed up so fully the response of the church that night after the five hard years of pilgrimage getting to that point. It read:

You will succeed,
not by ... your own strength,
but by my Spirit.
Obstacles as great as mountains
will disappear before you.
You will rebuild...
and as you put the last stone in place
the people will shout
'Beautiful, beautiful!'
(Zechariah 4.6,7; Good News Bible)

And how they did!

Everything in the opening service was in overdrive. All the lights were ablaze, the heating nearly overwhelmed us, and the organ was at full volume: plus. The bishop, who had been in office for less than a year and so was only beginning to get to know us, gave a marvellous welcoming word about the fact that we were witnesses to a miracle, and that we should be warned from scripture about the varied responses to miracles that we were likely to meet. Michael Baughen spoke with authority and gentle encouragement from Psalm 126.

To this day the whole event still has the power to bring me to tears with the sense of wonder and incredible relief of that never-to-be-forgotten night.

Principles

It had been a glorious, yet searching, experience. Although a venture of faith, it had also been, as I was to put it afterwards, 'the most sustained period of discouragement I have ever experienced!' It certainly felt as if the metal was being tested: which is why faith was needed — and given.

The church extension project also quickly became quite widely known. During the time we had had considerable exposure to the media. Not only had I been interviewed on the regional news programmes for both BBC and ITV, but reports of various gift days found their way into national newspapers. We were even featured in Money Mail. It was not long before other churches, often just about to launch into a project themselves, began to ask us for help and advice.

Eric, Richard, Jonathan and myself, often now joined by Terry Pratt, who had taken over as churchwarden from Richard, ran several weekends for leaders of such churches. We were regularly showing people round the building and telling them the story.

All of this forced us to reflect on our experience and to seek to identify the principles which had been important for us. Some of them were foundational to the way we began, others emerged on the way, further ones we stumbled across in the course of our journey.

In due course we identified eight in all.

First, we knew the importance of discovering God's will. We had been reassured as we faced the prospect of considerable expenditure, by the saying that 'God's work, done in God's way, never lacks

God's resources'. However, that is a double-edged saying. If the work was not of God we would be in serious trouble. Later I was to sense considerable anxiety from a few diocesan authorities because in the final issue they would have been left to pick up the pieces if things had gone wrong. The total cost of the project was not far off one year's income of the diocesan quota from *all* the churches in the diocese. Their anxiety was understandable. The primary attitude however was one of support and help.

Our first concern was to establish that the whole idea was of God. We gave time to prayer at the initial stage, seeking God's mind and will in what we were considering. We also gave careful consideration to other options, before we went further. When problems came we knew we would need to be sure that this was not some good idea of ours, but part of God's call to the church. Every step we took confirmed the rightness of what we were about to launch into. In prayer we sensed a witness of the Spirit. 'Follow your peace' is an old Quaker saying. That was how it felt. Even in the middle of later storms and batterings that quiet inner conviction that this was of God, and that he would see us through, never left us.

Second, we learnt the importance of involving the whole congregation, not only in the giving, but in the planning and deciding. By taking the whole church into our confidence we not only had the sense of the rightness of the project confirmed, but were assured of support from the start. It was only later that we saw how foolish it would have been to do otherwise. It would not be paid for by the church council membership alone: we needed the whole church to be involved in the giving at a level that would only happen if the members had had time to weigh up the whole idea and come to the same conviction we had that this was of God.

The Council of Jerusalem, as recorded in Acts chapter fifteen, where the leaders are having to make a fundamental theological decision ('Are Gentiles also heirs of the promises?'), was an important model for us. The whole church met to discuss; and the leaders listened to the Spirit speaking through the church. We could do no less.

Our third principle was to work from the basis of God's will rather than our resources. Our commitment was to discover what God wanted us to do. We were sure that once we knew that then we could trust him for all that would be needed to do it. The consequence of this was that we would be trusting God for the resources we needed. This did not mean that we used faith as an excuse for irresponsible spending. At one crucial decision point we faced the possibility of having to decide between a one- or a two-storey extension. It was Eric France who brought us the scripture from the Council of Jerusalem's conclusion: 'It seemed good to the Holy Spirit and to us not to lay upon you any other burden than these necessary things' (Acts 15.28). We chose the one-storey alternative.

It was tempting to go for the cheapest job possible but we knew that we and future generations would live to regret it. It would be a lack of faith, and an unwillingness to sacrifice, to take that course. Such an approach would have given us a short time enjoying not paying much, and a lifetime regretting we did not do a better job. By the grace of God we spent a (comparatively) short time in agony about the cost, and ever since have been delighted with what we now have to show for it.

In the fourth place we sought to apply gospel principles to practical problems. Rather than be frustrated by the fact that we were having to concern ourselves about buildings instead of getting on with the work of proclaiming the gospel and caring for the needy, we sought to apply and proclaim the gospel by the way we tackled our problems.

We had already discovered, when we stopped collecting money (even for others) while carol singing around the parish at Christmas, how puzzled parishioners were to find the church not out for their money. That gave us opportunity to point to the coming of Jesus, not the collecting of money, as the point of our singing. The same pattern was repeated on a larger scale in the building project. The fact that we were trusting God for the money, and making sacrifices ourselves, was pointing to the grace (the giving) of God which we had experienced.

One of the consequences of this approach was that when church members went to work after a gift day, or some other major event in the project, they found, like the early church, that 'we cannot help speaking about what we have seen and heard' (Acts 4.20). The opportunity to tell the good news of Jesus came naturally out of such conversations. A good number of people came to faith in this way during the period of building.

The fifth thing we did was to set the whole project in the wider context of the mission of the church. We certainly had never been a congregation that focused on buildings for their own sake. In that way we were fortunate to have had a building which I often described as 'nice'. It was perfectly pleasant, but had no great architectural merit and beauty in itself. That was to make our job so much easier than handling a church burdened by all the restrictions of being a beautiful building.

We soon realised that a building project can be bad for the health of a church. Inevitably you are putting secondary things (buildings) first. One or two frustrated church members did say to me in the course of the project, 'I'm fed up with hearing about buildings, buildings, buildings: we should be concentrating on preaching the gospel.' It was very understandable. However, after a few such remarks I learnt to answer them by pointing out that this would probably be the only major emphasis, at St Thomas's, on buildings this century. It would take four years. Four per cent of our effort as a church to improve the building where so much of our life took place was a reasonable emphasis. I usually added, 'I'm sorry you have hit that four per cent by being here now!'

Our sixth principle was to pray and work for opening the building free of debt. Several reasons lay behind this whole faith approach to the work.

First, we had no hidden reserves, so we needed the money to pay the bills. The only alternative would have been to take out loans (at a time of high interest rates) which would have only added to the cost. Second, we knew how much easier it is to find the money for something in order to have it, rather than after you have got it. We had heard too many stories of churches which had taken out a massive loan to do a whole building programme, only to discover that their subsequent income did not even

cover the interest payments. That was no way to
proclaim the greatness or generosity of God. Third,
we were convinced that we who had the vision
should pay for it to be completed. Again we knew
of too many situations where one generation
enjoyed a new building, and left the next one to
pay. Fourth, opening free of debt, gave us a specific
and limited time period in which to call the church
to the highest levels of sacrificial giving. Fifth, this
principle had obviously worked, and been blessed
by God, elsewhere.

*Our seventh principle of calling people to the
highest levels of sacrificial giving for a limited period*
(namely, up to the opening date only), arose
directly out of the prior commitment to open free of
debt. Jesus was our model in this whole approach to
giving. He gave all, and called others to do the
same as they followed him.

We saw how many fund-raising approaches relied
on sub-Christian motivation. Such things as raffles,
and sales of work, rely on the idea of getting
something (or, at least, the hope of something) for
your giving. Sponsored events depend heavily on
moral pressure, and using the leverage of personal
relationships to get people to part from their
money. Secular fund raising, like secular society, is
based on the principle of avoiding sacrifice. Our
intention was to encourage people to give, and give
sacrificially, after the pattern of Jesus's living. It
was certainly this that proclaimed the gospel to
those around us who saw what was going on. It also
strengthened the faith of all those involved because
we all had to step out in faith to give what we did.
Seeing God honour and bless that faith drew us to
him in praise, and renewed trust.

Our eighth principle was the immersion of the whole venture in prayer. That has already emerged in the story at the corporate level. We were also to discover just how important personal prayer was too. We discovered that all the targets which we produced were counter-productive. Even ones like 'a thousand pounds per wage earner', or 'the equivalent of a week's wages' had harmful side-effects. Those who should be giving more stopped at this lower level with a sense of achievement; those for whom it was right to give less felt they had failed.

In the end we abandoned all such targets, and discovered that there was only one reliable way to proceed. This was to urge everyone to turn to God in prayer. As we did that, we found God speaking to us about the giving he was calling us to. For some it meant, quite literally, doubling and doubling again what we were giving. For others, and there were some whom I had to counsel along these lines, they had to take the difficult path of stepping out in faith by giving absolutely nothing. That was their obedience and faith which God would honour in the project.

These eight principles guided us through this venture. We took time to pass them on to others, and still do today as other churches continue to ask for our help in their projects.

These principles can be summed up in the supreme goal of seeking to honour God by faith-filled obedience to him wherever he leads. That way proved costly, disturbing, and at times baffling. But we came through such testing rejoicing in his goodness, his generosity, his wisdom and his love.

Chapter Five

THE GIFT OF GIVING

The experience of the building had been exhilarating, exhausting, and very instructive. It also put us in the limelight and gave us a dangerous and unlooked for reputation of being 'a wealthy church'. In terms of the income of the congregation that simply was not true, but in terms of the generous giving of God's people we certainly had more resources than many. It was frequently said to us that our large staff was what promoted growth and stimulated giving. In fact, it was the giving which enabled us to add additional staff. We had certainly discovered just how important a firm financial base is to the growth of the church.

We were being invited to go to other churches and pass on the lessons we had learnt. Reflection was called for after all the action of the building project. We needed this for our own good, as well as to have something to say when we went. God had evidently been at work among us and I needed to discern why and how that had come about. The starting point was my own pilgrimage in this area of faith and giving.

Personal Preparation

Three particular experiences had prepared me for the challenge of the building project, and for the whole financial side of the life of the church.

First was the way in which my own father handled his financial relationship with me. As soon as I say that he was a stockbroker, pictures of a wealthy upbringing are likely to spring to the reader's mind. Though we were certainly never poor, life was really not like that.

My father had joined a stockbroking firm at the age of sixteen as a messenger boy. Over the years, by hard and reliable work, and with a gift of wisdom, he advanced in the firm until he became one of the partners. This was a double-edged blessing as it not only gave a full share in the profits, but also a full share in the losses. Some years those losses meant that there was little money coming in. My parents put a high value on their children's education and made considerable sacrifices for them. I was financed through public school, and later Cambridge University. So I was brought up in a home where sacrifices were made, and where little was spent on luxuries.

However, the formative thing for me was the way that my father handled my allowance at school, and especially at university. The occasions when I had overspent, or simply ran out of money, were anxious times. While I knew that I would be called on to give account for how I had spent my money, I also had an underlying confidence that if I asked for further help it would be forthcoming — not in any sense as the easiest thing to do — but because of his commitment to care for and support me. I am sure that this underlying confidence enabled me to begin tithing pocket money before I ever earned a wage. Thereafter, although often having felt called by God to go beyond that level, it has never presented any problems.

In this way my earthly father modelled for me the generosity of my heavenly Father. I did not find it difficult to trust him to provide what was needed: especially when it was for his work.

The second major influence on my attitude to finances within the church was my time as curate to Michael Baughen in Manchester. I saw him working out the principles of trusting God for the resources needed for his work. The church took on a £25,000 building project when (1966-8) a venture of that size was virtually unknown, certainly in the north of England, with a far from wealthy congregation. Michael had a steadfast and unshakeable faith that God would provide the money. Moreover, he took a vigorous approach to the whole matter of faith, and laid his own faith and reputation on the line.

The operation was built around the principle of opening free of debt. As the project proceeded it was clear that the final gift day, due on the Sunday before the new hall was to be opened, would be the make or break event. Several thousand pounds were still needed. Much thought, and prayer, and sacrifice, however, had gone into the run-up to that day. So much was given that the church had enough and some to spare for the work. It was a memorable experience.

There was one very surly parishioner who kept repeating to us throughout that project, 'You'll never do it, you'll never do it.' With some glee we went round after the final gift day to tell him what had happened. He obviously had already heard, because he greeted us with the jubilant shout, 'We've done it, we've done it!'

The experience of the building project in Manchester had a profound effect on me, and on my attitude to trusting God for the needs of his work.

The third experience that was part of my preparation was one particular gift day in the church in Wolverhampton.

We needed to tarmac the church car park which was a dust bowl in summer, and either a quagmire or skating rink in winter. To this end we had what we called the 'four hundred project' in which we aimed to give four hundred pounds to do this work. We took the step of faith of having the work done during the week leading up to the gift day. The bishop was coming to the evening service. It was a very big target for a small church at the end of the sixties, but having been through such things before I was not particularly anxious.

Not, that is, until after the morning service. Knowing the make-up of the congregation I knew that we needed most of the money in the morning. One third of the evening congregation (of under one hundred people) would be young people with few financial resources. A further third were partners of those who had come in the morning. A number of the remaining third had been at the morning service. The sources of giving were few indeed. Yet in the morning only seventy-two pounds was given. Ann and I were devastated.

We went for a walk along the canal side that afternoon and wrestled with the whole situation. We could not honestly see that we had made mistakes about the project being within the will of God. Nor could we doubt his faithfulness. Nor could we see any way in which the evening congregation could possibly make up the difference. We were caught: with no way to turn. Yet, by the end of our walk — and it was an agony we were in — we had come to two conclusions. Although we were convinced that there was no way in which the evening congregation could make up the difference, we also were convinced — with even greater strength — that there was no way that God would not be faithful to his Word, and honour his name.

In this frame of mind I went to the evening service. The bishop, sensing my concern, attempted to encourage me by saying 'Seventy-two pounds was a magnificent total this morning, if you were to achieve the same again, you would have done marvellously.' To me it was comforting with faint faith, and no help.

I had said that, as usual, I would announce the total at the end of the service. A number of people who had been in the morning service came back after the evening one simply to hear the total announced. Somehow I found myself at the front of the church speaking about something profound (probably giving out the notices!) when the treasurer came out of the vestry and held up a piece of paper. Everyone saw him, realised that he had the figure for the day, and went very quiet. The unusual thing about this situation was that this was the first (and last) time I ever went in front of a congregation to announce the total of a gift day without knowing myself what the figure was. I do not know how the treasurer felt as he walked down the aisle to hand to me that piece of paper. I know that I have never felt so exposed or alone. I could do nothing but open the folded paper, which I still have today, and say what was written on it. I had no plans for what I would say. I certainly was not going to try and explain it away.

There was no need. I seemed to be the only one whose faith was faint. On the paper was written: 'Morning £72: Evening £352: Total £424.' Wow! I had to suppress tears of joy, and praise, thankfulness and relief, simply to read it out. The joy of the church did the rest.

The vital part of this event for Ann and me was that agonising walk along the canal tow path. At the time I felt angry that God was making life so difficult. With hindsight we now know he was not doing that. He was making us strong. The metal of our faith was being tested, and having some more impurities burnt out. It was a crucible experience. It is important to see that it was the struggle of the canal-side walk, rather than the ecstasy of the result in church, that wrote God's faithfulness into our experience of life. True Christian success grows out of weakness, failure, and despair: it is tough enough to survive.

We were also learning that God's preference seems always to be to act at the eleventh hour!

Creating a Giving Environment

In learning about giving I had established the personal agenda that God had been working on. I also needed to reflect on the lessons we had learnt as a church. We were able to look back over a number of years during which giving had been growing well ahead of the growth of the church, or the income of its members. Although the gift day in 1972, and the Church Extension Project, stood out like mountain peaks in that story, there was another side to our giving that was no less striking.

Just as we began the building project we discovered that the giving had doubled over the previous three years. It was not easy to explain why this was so. During that period (1973-5) we had no special needs, and held no gift days. We did nothing different about the way we handled our giving. The church had only grown by ten per cent during that period.

It was not until the Urban Church Project survey done in 1978 by David Wasdell that we saw what was happening.

It was all to do with *worthship,* which is the ancient Anglo-Saxon word for worship. The church was expressing, through its giving, the worth of the life of the church they were involved in. As we thought further we identified three aspects of that 'worthship' which was being expressed.

1 Grace

Soon after the Operation Eyesore gift day of 1972, I was invited to speak at another church on the subject of giving. I wanted to take one or two members of the church with me who would speak from their experience about their motivation to give. The problem was that we deliberately handled the giving in such a way that none of the clergy knew whether, or how much, anyone gives. I went to the treasurer and asked him if he could suggest two people who, from his knowledge of the giving, he thought would have something to say. He did, and I invited them to be involved, which they agreed to do.

I had asked the treasurer to suggest people who he thought would be practising tithing (giving a tenth of their income). When the three of us met to plan what we would say I asked these two men what led them to practise tithing. 'Practise what?' was the response of both of them. They did not seem to have heard the word. When I said it meant a tenth, I could see both of them doing quick sums in their heads to work out if that was what they were giving. When pressed further, both of them, who were new to the Christian faith, were saying they had been giving because of what they had received from God. Both of them were saying 'I simply wanted to give back to God'. His love for them was their inspiration for giving.

The giving of these two men was the response of the believer to the grace of God.

Certainly the apostle Paul saw it this way. When he was writing to the Corinthian church about giving you might have expected him to begin commending the example of the Macedonians by saying 'I want you to know about the giving of the churches in Macedonia'. However, he does not say that. Rather, he says, 'I want you to know about the grace that God has given the Macedonian churches' (2 Corinthians 8.1). Paul is pointing to the root cause of the church's giving; namely, God's giving to them.

When I am asked what I would do with a church that has a low level of giving, I begin at this point. I would not want to berate it for not giving sacrificial-ly, but I would want to make sure that the grace of God was getting through to them. Weak-looking vegetables in the garden are usually the consequence of soil that has not been fed. The nourishment in God's vineyard is his grace: his generous overflowing love and goodness. It needs to be getting through to his people. So, when giving is limited, I would begin to work on the church's limited experience of the grace of God. As I sometimes put it: *if the giving is poor, give God's people more.*

Grace must flow. It happens in a multitude of ways. God's love, and goodness, comes through the teaching of his word. It comes to us through the sacraments, through the love and generosity of others in the fellowship of the church. It comes to us as we pray, and by the working of the Holy Spirit. God's mercy and life come to us in repentance, through pastoral care and in personal relationships.

This, I have come to see, is the priestly role of ministering God's love and mercy, presence and power, to his people. It is the calling of all of us in leadership in the church to communicating God's life and mercy and love to his people.

2 Vision

The second factor we detected in the giving environment among us was vision. Giving will be the response of those who experience the grace of God. But it will not necessarily be channelled into any particular part of God's vineyard, unless faith is stimulated by a vision of the purposes of God in that particular church or venture.

People will make great sacrifices once they see what they are being called to make sacrifices for, and are convinced of the worth of what is being done. That was certainly our experience in the building project. In some ways it was even more evident in the 1972 gift day, when we were giving for the churchyard. There can hardly be a less inspiring cause, yet the church was able to see beyond that and was motivated to give out of love for God, and out of zeal for his kingdom. Re-ordering the churchyard was symbolic of the church opening up to the community around us. That motivated us.

The church often attempts to motivate people by the blunt instrument of moral pressure: what someone has called 'mustage and oughtery'. What actually motivated us is a cause worth dying for. Tony Campolo once said that 'young people are made for heroism not comfort'. That is true for most human beings. The most surprising people will cheerfully make great sacrifices, if they are fired by the worth of what is being done. Even the atheist philosopher, Jean-Paul Sartre, acknowledged this truth about humanity when he said, 'No man is happy unless he has something worth dying for.' What folly then that so much of the emphasis on giving within the Christian church is concerned to reduce any element of sacrifice. The 'if-everyone-gives-a-little' approach usually leads to no one giving anything much. It signals to people that this venture is not worth much. They then respond by obeying the instructions and giving just that ... not much!

I have come to see this as one of the evidences of the failure of nerve of Western Christianity. To break out of it involves us in a prophetic ministry, as we spell out the purposes of God. This is an important control on any venture. If the vision is not of God we will find that the giving is not either.

The Church of England has a marvellous phrase for describing someone who is given responsibilities in a diocese when there is no bishop. The person is called 'the guardian of the spiritualities'. That is the role of leadership in a local church or Christian venture. It has to do with articulating the vision for all those involved.

3 Belonging

It was our fellowship groups that the Urban Church Project survey identified as the single greatest cause of the doubling of giving in the mid-1970s. Church members had a heightened sense of belonging by being in one of the groups. It showed in the giving.

Later we were to experience this principle working in reverse. As so often happens we learnt more in the hard times than we did in the joyful ones.

In the mid-1980s, we went through a difficult time which included financial problems. One positive outcome was a new understanding of a sense of belonging. People were saying that they felt they did not belong. Since then we have identified four elements in a sense of belonging which had a considerable effect on the level of people's giving. Here are the ingredients.

First, we all need to know and be known. We need to feel that someone notices us and cares if we are not there. If others not only notice my absence, but value my presence, and say so, so much the better. For many churches this has been the effect of home groups. In them we feel we belong.

Significantly, during this time, we had actually abolished the role of supporting fellowship leader. It was showing in our accounts.

Second, is the need to hear and be heard by the leadership. We need to know, and catch the vision of, the leaders; and also to feel that our views, ideas, vision (and, yes, complaints) are heard. As the church grows the members need to have a relationship with those whom they perceive to be in leadership. We were not doing that very well.

Third, is the need to be able to value the contribution we can make to the whole operation. This is where the church often works on a far too passive understanding of pastoral care. Such an approach can be characterised as an are-you-sitting-comfortably style. The trouble is that the healthy Christian does not want to do a lot of sitting comfortably. Could it be that (if they are Anglicans) those words spoken over them in baptism ('fight valiantly under the banner of Christ against sin, the world and the devil') have actually got through? Maybe they are restless because they want to be up and doing. Putting people to work in the kingdom of God is a proper and vital part of pastoral care.

Fourth, is the need to own the purpose of the whole venture. Increasingly I have come to see that the whole membership of the church needs to assent to the direction in which the church is going. This includes not only contributing to achieving the goal, but also participating in shaping and forming that direction and vision.

Certainly we have found it possible, even in a church with over a thousand worshippers, to work as a whole body in discerning the direction and priorities God is giving us. When every member feels that he or she has participated in the shaping of that vision, and is then called to contribute financially, a response is usually forthcoming.

All of these four factors in a healthy sense of belonging come about through effective pastoral work. Practical care of each person is needed in order for a sense of belonging to be evident.

So grace, vision and a sense of belonging are vital ingredients we have discovered as essential to the creation of a giving environment. We have also found that simple and effective structures are a vital part of mobilising the giving of the church.

Structure

Though changing the structures will not create healthy giving, such sacrifices are unlikely to find expression without a simple means of channelling them. The system we have operated for over twenty years was instituted by my predecessor and remains substantially unchanged. It is as follows:

Once a year (in November) we have *Commitment Sunday*. In preparation for that several things happen.

A letter is sent to every regular worshipper setting out the financial needs of the church for the coming year, reminding people of some of the principles of Christian giving, and inviting them to take three actions. First, everyone is encouraged to pray: both about their own giving to God, and also about the response of the whole church to the financial situation. Second, enclosed in the letter is a *commitment card*. On it there is space for us to say how much we plan to give per week/month/year, and whether we wish to covenant that amount. Third, everyone is invited to bring the card to church on Commitment Sunday, and to bring it forward in a special act of giving.

In this simple way, everyone is encouraged not just to have vague intentions or even marvellous plans, but rather to make a decision and act.

On the Sunday before Commitment Sunday, we preach on some aspect of giving by way of preparation. We never preach about giving on Commitment Sunday or on a gift day, for the simple reason that by then it is too late. If people are going to give sacrificially they need time to think and prepare and plan for such giving. So *teaching*, a *simple form* to complete, and *prayer* are the elements that have served us well in providing that structure or channel through which giving can be expressed.

The commitment card has two sections, one for the church and one for missionary work, so decisions about what percentge of our income goes to missionary work is made by the whole membership of the church, not by the church council.

Spirituality

Our experience of giving has left us in no doubt that it is an important way in which we express our attitude of love and obedience to God. More recently we have come to see that this is an important place in which the spiritual battle takes place. Inevitably this is so in a materialistic culture. We are now alert to the fact that this is an area where we can expect spiritual attack. We have been learning to have our weapons ready. There are three in particular that we value highly.

The *scriptures* are the basis of our teaching and have a dynamic power all of their own. The word of God is a life-giving force that motivates the spirit of the believers. We have already mentioned *prayer*, and our encouragement to individuals to come before God and discover his will about their giving. Not least during our building project we found this to be the key. This one truth has been the most vital ingredient: that when the people of God pray about their giving all heaven is let loose.

A further element of the spirituality of giving is what I call the charismatic dimension: that is, the work of *the Holy Spirit* in giving people the gift of giving and removing the obstacles to such grace. In so many ways we are captives to the gods of this age. Only the Holy Spirit can touch us to the core and release repentance about our selfishness or unbelief about money. He alone can break the bonds of a materialistic culture that holds the church in the sub-standard captivity of hobby-giving and release God-inspired and overflowing generosity. He alone can reveal to us our material and security idols and break their power as we make costly choices before God. So in all this we have sought the power of the Holy Spirit to set us free to give. We seek to release the grace of God on a whole believing community so that God will be glorified.

Chapter Six

ACTIVE SERVICE

There had been two inspirations behind the church extension project. One was to create space for Sunday services, the other had been to provide suitable accommodation for our mid-week service of the community.

When we began the project we did not need those extra seats for most Sundays in the year, but the growth of the church led us to take the step of faith to provide room for those whom we believed God would add to the church. The desire to serve the local community was part of the fruit of the spiritual renewal we had earlier experienced. It was for this reason that most of the extension of the church building had been for week-time activities. These two concerns were interlocking, for we saw church growth not as an end in itself but as a means to the end of working for the coming of the kingdom of God, and the forwarding of Christ's mission here on earth. Church growth without mission will always end up in empire building.

As we returned to our new building, we were eager to find how God would lead us out in that mission. Not that our service of others began with the re-opening of the new St Thomas's: God had

been preparing us in the previous years for the
work that was to come.

First Steps Backwards

Our first steps into mission, after I became vicar,
seemed at the time to be backward ones. One of the
earliest effects of renewal was the closure of a series
of inherited church activities.

In the space of eighteen months we saw all four
uniformed organisations (cubs, scouts, brownies,
and guides) close. In this same period, our robed
choir and our annual garden party also ceased.
Some missionary prayer meetings, and the men's
and women's Bible study groups, also decided to
stop so that the members could concentrate on the
new supporting fellowships. Initially I tried hard to
find new leaders to succeed those who wanted to
stand down. Such leaders were not forthcoming.
When that happened, the existing leaders and I had
to make the decision to close the activity. Partly this
had to do with a lack of vision for the organisations
themselves, and partly because all our best leaders
were now involved in making supporting fellowships work. I felt as if I was presiding over the
biggest decline in church life that Crookes Church
(as it is usually called in the community) had ever
known. It was not easy to let go, as it felt like
failure, but in doing so I learnt some important
lessons.

A Waiting Time

In the early years of the 1970s, with very limited
facilities, and a preoccupation with personal spir-

itual renewal, the primary calling to us was to establish fellowship groups. The church seemed to be in retreat from engagement with the community, though what was happening was very important. The Holy Spirit was ploughing up our way of doing things and in that fertile soil planting the seeds of new ways of serving God.

We had to dare to wait for God's timing in this.

Michael Baughen had set me a clear example in this while I was working with him in Manchester. Of all the things dear to his heart I knew, from the day I arrived, how keen he was to see a flourishing men's group. Yet, man of great drive and energy though he was, he did nothing. Or rather, he appeared to do nothing. In truth he was waiting — for God's moment. It was not until three years later, just as I was leaving, that he took any action. One day a young man turned up on his doorstep enquiring about the Christian faith. Michael spent time with him, and several other men whom this man brought along. Then, in what seemed like no time at all, Michael recognised this man as the leader of the men's group. So it proved to be. A remarkably flourishing group emerged in a matter of months just when most men's groups were in terminal decline. Watching Michael, I learnt that waiting for God's moment is the fastest way to get things done; though it is not easy, or readily understood.

Getting Going

It was the church-shaking gift day in 1972 that first prompted us to take action to mobilise the whole membership of the church in ministry. You will recall the sense we had of having hit the jackpot with that day. We were eager to apply the principles of that gift day to every area of the life of the church. Having focused on the stewardship of our money, we turned our attention to what are often called 'time and talents'. What we did was to hold a Gifts gift day.

Like the Commitment Sunday we hold each year about our giving of money, we invited people on Gifts gift day, to fill up a card saying what they saw as the gifts God had given them, and the ministry that they were willing to exercise in the life of the church.

Bezalel was a great inspiration to us in this. It was recorded of him:

> Then Moses said to the Israelites, 'See, the Lord, has chosen Bezalel son of Uri, the son of Hur, of the tribe of Judah, and he has filled him with the Spirit of God, with skill, ability and knowledge in all kinds of crafts — to make artistic designs for work in gold, silver and bronze, to cut and set stones. to work in wood and to engage in all kinds of artistic craftsmanship.
> (Exodus 35.30-33)

We took our first, faltering steps in helping everyone to see that to be a Christian is to be called to active service, however varied may be the ways in which God calls us to exercise that ministry.

Good Foundations

The whole emphasis of our ministry in the early part of the seventies was on resourcing the renewal we were experiencing. Many of our most gifted leaders were involved in the leading of supporting fellowships.

We also drew some of our most committed members into a worship team. We deliberately called it that to indicate that the task was not primarily one of making music, though that was involved, but of leading worship. To this end we appointed John Goepel as director of music. The text we used on that occasion was a marvellous verse I had come across from the Old Testament. It read:

Then Cheneniah was put
in charge of the music —
for he understood it.
(1 Chronicles 15.22)

What a marvellous way for deciding who should do which jobs!

Under the leadership of David Hughes we also developed a counselling ministry based on the pattern known as Wholeness Through Christ. A regular flow of church members went on retreats to receive prayer-counselling themselves, and were thereby equipped to counsel others.

During this time we gave attention to the organisation surrounding our Sunday services. We not only changed the title of sidesmen to stewards, we also gave it a high profile in the life of the church, and encouraged those who were new to the church to become stewards as a first step into ministry. This meant that often those greeting us at the door were the newest members. It enabled them to feel involved, and helped us to get to know them and to begin to discover their gifts and abilities. Under a series of dedicated and able leaders this has become one of the foundational ministries in the church. Indeed such is the skill that has been developed and passed down that when the Billy Graham mission was held in Sheffield in 1985 it was our stewarding team that handled the nightly crowd of between twenty and forty thousand people. The change of title made it easier to have women as well as men (without needing to call the women 'stewardesses'!).

We also introduced an overhead projector, and an amplification system, into the worship and these needed manning at every service. Much work was put into training people to operate these systems effectively. That continuing training has provided us with great back-up. Such ministries are working best when nobody notices them.

In these, and other ways, the foundations were being laid for an efficient functioning of the church that was to prove vital in the years to come as the growth of the church increased.

Charity Begins at Home

Not only were good structures being set up for the administration of our Sunday services, and for the whole work of the church; the middle years of the 1970s were also a time to lay new foundations to some of the basic pastoral work of the church.

The Sunday work with children was in the process of hand-over from those who had served the work faithfully over many years — especially the indefatigable Aunty Doris who had taught in the Sunday schools for over fifty years — to young mothers and teachers who had more recently joined the church. Here again we were seeking to find new ways of handling the communication of our faith to our children. The work was moving from a classroom to a family setting, with a desire to help the children to experience God as well as to learn the truths of scripture. As a result of a visit by Anne Watson, from St Michael-le-Belfry in York, this change of style was more firmly established, initially under the leadership of our parish worker Adele Fox, and the Sunday schools renamed Sonship.

Under David Hughes, and later Paul Wells, we ran a small but spiritual youth fellowship for the teenage children of church family members.

Vital though good administrative structures and a spiritual ministry to the children and young people of the church are, there was an eagerness for more. Those who had experienced renewal were wanting to break out of the passenger mentality of church life, and were asking what they could do. The desire to serve, and especially to serve beyond the bounds of internal church activities, vital though they are, was on the increase. Throughout this time 'ministry' was having an increasing emphasis in the life of the church. This began to show in a number of ways.

Kathleen France had already led the way, having pioneered a very effective playgroup which was started before I arrived. Kathleen was very skilled in this, and for some time was involved in playgroup work at the national level. The group has continued over the years to have dedicated lay leadership from within the church family. It was the beginning of our work with young families. It now functions three times a week.

Sue Laughlin later started a Mother and Toddler group which began to draw some mothers who were not members of the church.

Stepping Out

Our buildings were increasingly frustrating this call to serve. Nonetheless new outward-looking developments began to emerge as the prospect of a new building loomed. Not surprisingly the pace quickened once it was open.

These new developments were to teach us much and to lead us into new ways of serving the community, and also into a fresh way of understanding how 'ministry' works in the life of the church. Four particular developments illustrate some of the lessons we were learning.

1 The Re-cycling Project

Arthur Champion was an energetic and engaging young man with a high commitment to Christ, to pot-holing and matters of conservation. He was on the PCC during the building project and came to us at one meeting with a marvellous idea that he had had. He thought it would be good if the church could mount a project to re-cycle bottles, and newsprint, and so raise money for the building project. The PCC made an interesting response. They agreed that it was a great idea, and told Arthur to get on and organise it, but they made one stipulation. The money was not to go to the project, despite the vast sums we needed. They were clear that this would breach our principle of not seeking financial help from the local community, even though it was in the form of discarded bottles and paper. 'Go ahead, but give the money away,' the

PCC was saying.

Out of this came a major operation which, at its peak, resulted in close on two thousand pounds a year being sent, via Tear Fund, to self-help projects in the third world.

Perhaps in preparation for the later local ecumenical project with the Baptists, we now established the (as far we knew, first ever) joint Anglican-Whitbread bottle bank, behind the Ball Inn!

Once a month a newspaper skip arrived at the church car park and was often full to overflowing as word got round the community. Three things were being achieved at the same time. Those most in need in the world were receiving financial help; the cause of conservation was being advanced, and members of the church were establishing new relationships with people in the community. A good number of members of the church established a collection round in their street. Once a month they went to collect bottles and newspapers from neighbours and then take their collection off to the paper skip, and the bottle bank.

One of the most important things about the re-cycling project was the relationship it had to the church as an organisation. Here was a work that the church, as an organisation, had not initiated, nor, in the final issue, was it responsible for. Someone within the church had the idea and was given support and authority to recruit workers within the church, but it remained his responsibility.

The re-cycling project exactly paralleled the vision behind the building project. Here was an integrated operation — combining spiritual, social, and ecological issues in one operation — that was turning the attention of the church outwards to the community around. It was a significant pointer to the way ahead.

However, I must complete the picture. Five or six years later Arthur moved. We never found someone with Arthur's particular sense of call and vision to head the work. Then the pub unilaterally closed the bottle bank. Finally, we had vandal problems with the paper skip, which resulted in complaints from neighbours, especially when some local youths attempted to set it on fire.

By now we were accustomed to, indeed quite skilled at, allowing things to die.

2 Mor, and More, and Moore

With this experience of lay ministry under our belt we were more quickly ready for a similar pattern to be worked out in a very different area.

Shirley Moore (the daughter of Ernest Renner, who had been the churchwarden when I arrived) had been divorced and subsequently moved back to Crookes, with her two teenage sons. In the fellowship of the church Shirley found love and acceptance, a renewal of her faith, and a deep sense of God's acceptance and his healing of all the pain of the experience.

Out of the blue, Shirley felt that God was telling her to get the divorced people of the church together and to help them to support each other. She felt out of her depth, and came to me in some anxiety about what she should do. I sensed the call of God in the situation and encouraged her to act. So the MOR group was formed. The name MOR not only had obvious links with Shirley's name, but was used as the title of the group, standing for the Mending of Relationships. It was to become a haven for those who came into the church recovering from the hurt and rejection and self-doubt that so often follow in the wake of divorce.

What we had learnt through the re-cycling project about lay initiative in ministry, and about an outward-looking concern, was invading the internal pastoral work of the church. Although it was not a group set up by the church in an official or organisational sense, we soon incorporated it into our pastoral structures and we treat it as one of our fellowship groups.

3 Mother and toddler growth

Moving back into the new St Thomas's allowed us to develop the mother and toddler groups in a way that had hitherto been impossible because of our lack of space. The church itself had experienced a baby boom at the end of the seventies, and again at the end of the building project. Moreover, as more young couples were buying up the houses in the community and starting their married life in Crookes, the number of mothers with toddlers steadily increased.

The leaders are committed to advance the whole work through prayer, which often lasts several hours at a time as they seek God's blessing and direction. They have sought to integrate practical service with the spiritual lessons we were learning as a church; indeed sometimes they have been ahead of the rest of the church. Increasingly time has been given to prayer and to waiting on God for his leadership of the whole work. Listening to God, intercession, keeping relationships within the team 'in the light', have all been important elements. The leaders were learning to minister the grace of God to each other before they sought to do so to those who came.

This commitment by the leaders naturally affects the whole style of the daily sessions. Newcomers are quickly welcomed, and in the friendly and caring setting the whole person is cared for. Although most of those who come are not church members a pastoral and spiritual ministry is exercised in a relaxed and informal way. Practical help, a listening ear, counselling, prayer for healing, and leading people to faith, all find expression in the hubbub of the daily sessions. The love of Christ is being communicated.

One couple, not church-goers, experienced the trauma of premature still-birth while on holiday on the Continent. The mother and toddler groups clubbed together to raise over five hundred pounds to enable the couple to get the body back home for burial. They asked to come to a Sunday service to express their thanks. It was a moving testimony to God's love. A number of children have experienced healing from such ailments as asthma and a prolonged bout of headaches. One mother, who was drawn to faith as a result of the love that she experienced, has now started a keep fit group. In this group she not only helps people with physical fitness but with spiritual health too. Her sister-in-law has now come to faith: due largely to the rapid clearing up, as a result of prayer for healing, of a serious burn on her child's body.

Not surprisingly, with these facilities and this level of commitment, it is one of the most sought-after mother and toddler groups (somewhat a misnomer because men are numbered among their ranks now as well) in town. Four groups meet each week, drawing over one hundred mothers and over one hundred and fifty toddlers. We now see this as a primary mission area. God has given us, through the sacrifice of many, a mission field well inside our own doors.

As with the re-cycling project, we were seeing the integration of the spiritual and the practical, turning our attention outwards to the needs of those who were not members of the church, and giving church members freedom and encouragement to get on with the vision that they had for this work.

We were also learning that a ministry grows and develops as new leaders emerge. Our support had to change as the nature of the work changed: it was important not to put inappropriate constraints on those wanting to develop new elements in the work.

4 Harvest

John Lovell (who became churchwarden in 1986), had come to faith through the work of Patrick Coghlan in the late 1970s. John immediately learnt to apply his faith in a radical way to the whole of his living — including the publicity firm that he owned and ran. John lived in a comfortable family-sized house in a pleasant suburb of the city. In 1983 he sensed the Lord telling him not to become wrongly attached to his house. More than this he received a vision for a coffee and gift shop on the main road in Crookes. It was a radical step because it would involve selling his house, buying a shop in Crookes, and probably living in a flat above it. When John came to me I sensed with him that this was of God and that he should proceed.

Soon enough a shop on a splendid corner site became available and John moved to purchase it. It was to be called Harvest. The last five years have seen hundreds of local people come through its doors, and often find more than just food. A full-time manager is now employed, but the shop depends upon a considerable number of church family members helping with the cooking and preparation of food, and with serving meals.

The shop has faced many ups and downs, the most severe of which came in 1985. It had been founded on the principle of being of value to the community. One of the agreed tests of this was financial viability. Harvest had been losing money over the previous six months and so, with great reluctance, the decision was made to close it. We announced the fact on the second Sunday of March that year. It so happened that, in church at that service, was a couple from a nearby church whose ears pricked up at the announcement. The wife was a training officer for the Wimpy fast food chain. They went home, and considered the whole matter together in prayer. The result was that she resigned her well-paid job, with fine prospects, and became full-time manager.

Harvest was closed for just one month, and bounced back soon after it was re-opened. It has been through another difficult time since this manager left, with her husband, to work in Tonga. However, it is now under new management and flourishing again. In the difficult times it has been tempting to say the church would take it on in an official, legal, and financial sense. We have managed to avoid this to date, which has been healthy for the church and Harvest alike.

John was to experience God's care for his servants in two marvellous ways as far as his own accommodation needs were concerned. It quickly became apparent that he would not be able to live in the flat over the shop. It was not physically possible at first, and before long the room was needed as an enlarged kitchen. However, a couple in the church offered him a home with them.

The original idea for the shop was that it would not only be a coffee shop and restaurant, but would also be a gift shop. Although this did not happen it did lead John into further experience of God's provision. As part of his research about possible gift items he visited Liz Beer because he had heard about some patchwork which she had. Liz was a teacher and was then leading our worship team. One of the consequences of being in a large church is that you do not know everyone. Neither knew each other.

No sale was agreed, but a friendship developed, and they are now married. With Liz owning her own home, the Lord provided much more than the accommodation needs for a man who had dared to sell his home in obedience to God.

Previous developments had already pointed us in the direction of releasing church members to see themselves as the church, and so to get on with the vision they had. Here we took a step further in encouraging the development of a major work involving considerable financial investment which was independent of the church as an organisation. We were learning to see the church in two quite distinct ways. As an organisation it has a clearly defined legal and financial structure. Harvest was outside this. At the same time the church, in its fullest sense, is the body of believers. Harvest was fully part of the church in that sense.

Crookes Endowed School

Ever since 1735 Crookes had had a school: in its first years it was held in labourers' cottages. In 1791 the Crookes Endowed School was built — at a cost of £100. It adjoins the church and churchyard; or rather the church and churchyard adjoin it, as they came some fifty years after the school was built.

By 1969, good though the school was, its numbers had fallen to under one hundred and it was about to close. The church made plans for the demolition of the building and the construction of a church hall and vicarage on the site. That was the £40,000 building project which the church had in mind when I was chosen as the new vicar. By the time I arrived the whole scheme had been abandoned because the school was not then going to close.

However, early in 1981, within three months of the re-opening of the new St Thomas's, it was announced that the school would close at the end of the summer term that year. This decision could hardly have come at a worse time. We did not want another building project. In any case it is one thing to build with a specific purpose in mind, but quite another to find yourself considering the purchase of a building with no very clear idea about how to use it.

When the church was re-ordered, we made the worship area visible to all who came. We did this by having windows in the screen at the back of the worship area which practically everyone who comes into the building needs to pass. This visibility of the worship area was intended to be a sign that God is the focus and inspiration of all that goes on. For the re-ordered school building we sensed that God was saying, 'We are the temple of the living God' (2 Corinthians 6.16). We understood this to mean that God's presence would be indicated not by a room, a chapel or whatever, but by the involvement of Christians in the activities (both Christian and secular) that took place there.

With the opening, in 1982, of the Crookes Endowed Centre (as we had decided to call it) we were launched into a new dimension of service for which we were ill prepared. We certainly saw the building as a gift from God to be used to serve the community around us. However, we had the building before we had a clear grasp of how best to use it.

At an important practical level we were able to provide facilities for the local community. Part of the building is let to a very active rights and advice centre which many people have found a great help with housing, social benefits and other matters. The upstairs part of the building is in permanent use by Adult Education. Classes are held covering a wide range of subjects and activities. We also let rooms for social and other purposes to groups and individuals, although the number of available sessions is continually decreasing.

Half of the downstairs space has been turned into a youth centre with a games hall, craft area, coffee lounge and youth leader's office. These facilities enabled us to develop our youth work quite considerably. As a result we were able, in 1982, to take on a full-time youth worker. Steve Williams, a member of the church who had just completed his teacher training, began the work.

It has since been carried on and developed by Steve Lee. We had supported Steve and Di Lee, a Sheffield couple, in the nine years they had been on mission service in Lima, Peru. They had started two congregations, and a leather work for the unemployed youth of the shanty towns. Under Steve's leadership teams of church members have been established and they are running five growing groups designed for the 11-18 year-olds.

The building has also provided essential overflow facilities for our children's work on Sundays. It could hardly have survived without this space. The centre is certainly much used, with more than 35,000 people passing through its doors in 1987.

Crookes Endowed Centre, or CEC, as it is now known, mirrors the growing vision within the church to be a servant community, and is a sign to local people of that care. As such it has expressed our obedience to God in forwarding the mission of his Son.

Much good has come out of the centre, though it is doubtful whether we have made the best use of these facilities yet. It has been another learning situation as we have sought to discover God's will. However, there are solid gains.

Strands and Strains

The development of clearly spiritual ministries has taken place alongside our service to the community through the Crookes Endowed Centre. These are not the only elements in our service but they are the dominant ones. Much has been achieved, though there is much we have not yet resolved.

There is always a tension between these *charismatic* and *institutional* expressions of service. Our desire and goal is to avoid them becoming opposed to each other and being torn apart. We seek to discover how these two strands can be more effectively woven together. That is our vision.

The tension is between the inward and outward aspects of the church's life. When we first developed supporting fellowships the result was the collapse of a number of church activities. Those ministries have now begun again in more appropriate ways, but the tension remains, expressed often in pressure on the time people have available. A weekly involvement in a fellowship and a ministry, and possibly a third evening for leaders' meetings, is a heavy commitment. We have sometimes thought of turning our ministry teams into fellowship groups ('fellowship on the job'), but have not yet seen that as the way ahead. It is a tension that remains in the midst of a situation where much fellowship and much ministry are thriving.

Chapter Seven

MOBILISING AN ARMY

The new developments in which the church was serving the community did not happen by accident. They were the fruit of much thought, and prayer, hard work and constant review. Our goal had been to mobilise the church for the work of the kingdom in our day. We had to take risks, and to learn from our mistakes: which you cannot do until you admit you have made them!

Motivated by Grace

The upheaval of the period of decline in church activities which took place in the early seventies led me both to heart searching, and back to the scriptures for some answers to the dilemmas. One passage in particular crystalised a number of principles, though I was finding them repeated often in the life and ministry of Jesus. It comes at the end of chapter four in Luke's gospel. There we read:

> At daybreak Jesus went out to a solitary place. The people were looking for him and when they came to where he was, they tried to keep him from

leaving them. But he said, 'I must preach the good news of the kingdom of God to the other towns also, because that is why I was sent.' (Luke 4.42—44)

First, Jesus was able to say 'no'. What could be better than to stay in a community receptive to his teaching and healing ministry? Yet he did so because his attention was not on what those around him thought he should be doing, but on the call of God. This was a great encouragement to me to let go of activities that had ceased to inspire or motivate the church in service. Before I was ordained I had written in an article that 'Christendom is littered with the organisational relics of a working of God in a former generation.' Now I was having to act on the implications of that statement.

Second, Jesus was not motivated by moral pressure, but the Father's will. Clearly Jesus was free of such pressures from others; at the same time he was peculiarly sensitive to the will of the Father. I realised that there was a hidden agenda behind the sense of failure, which some people were feeling about the closure of all these activities. It seemed as if the church was motivated by moral pressure rather than God's call. The nature of this hidden agenda came to me in visual form. There was a mental checklist that some had at the back of their minds which read like this:

'The church must be seen to be..' and there followed a list. It included such things as doing youth work, and caring for the elderly, carol singing and raising money for charity, plus a hundred and one other things.

Jesus did not seem to work that way. Jesus has

only one item on his agenda. 'My food is to do the will of him who sent me and to finish his work' (John 4.34). That certainly satisfied him, so much so that the disciples thought he must have eaten. It satisfied me too. I decided that I would try to lead the church to dare to re-write its agenda of oughts to fit in with the lifestyle of Jesus. Then it would read:

'The church ought to ... do the will of God whether others see, or understand, it or not!'

It was an enormously liberating insight, but it involved costly changes. We were attempting to move the whole basis of ministry from works to grace, from duty to the call of God. Such changes involve spiritual battle. For me it meant letting go of other people's expectation that the vicar should keep everything going.

You're in the Army Now!

We were convinced that every believer had a calling, and gifts, and a ministry from God that he or she should be exercising. This might not necessarily be in a church organisation, but it would be part of the call to know and show God. We talked about a 'hospital-to-barracks' style of church life. We meant that, although many of us come to faith at a time of weakness and trouble, God is not intending to leave us in that state. He intends to make us whole, and fit, and able to bear fruit for him. On entering the church it may function towards us as a hospital, but the time will come when we need to hear God's call and know that we are in the army (of God) now.

We were looking for ways of calling the whole church into active service in that army. Our first steps, through the Gifts gift day held in 1973, were faltering ones, but crucial to our learning how this could be done.

Learning the Hard Way

Even before we had held the Gifts gift day we were aware of problems. By the time the day, and all the follow up work involved, was completed those problems were clearer still.

First, we were overwhelmed. Many did complete and return one of the Gifts gift day cards: indeed too many. This is where we ran into a problem that was frequently to defeat us in subsequent attempts to make a reality of every-member ministry. We had more responses than we could deal with. We also discovered that it was one thing to process one or two (or even five) hundred cards saying how much people will be giving (you either send them a box of envelopes, or a standing order, or a convenant form). However, when we came to processing close on two hundred ministry cards we realised that it would mean two hundred visits, usually taking a whole evening, in order to talk through with each person what they had put on the card, and to work out what he or she could be doing in the service of God.

These visits often uncovered all sorts of needs, which were more immediately important than what someone was doing in the life of the church. That simply aggravated the situation. Some people were not seen for months, or even a year. That in itself signalled just the opposite of what we were trying to say. Some felt ignored, put to the bottom of the list, and not valued within the church. 'You're getting round to the dregs now' was sometimes how I, and other staff members, were greeted. It was under-standable; but painful to us to be so greeted when we had been using every spare minute visiting such people.

Second, we were under staffed. Another problem was that we did not have enough leaders to visit those who had filled up the forms. That was a two-fold problem. We had not anticipated the size of the response, so had not trained others, though it is doubtful whether, at that stage in the life of the church, such non-staff leaders would have been accepted.

Third, we found that gifts do not easily fit on forms. It was very much easier to express financial giving on a small card than to say in a word or two what you see as your gift or ministry.

Fourth, we encountered much self-doubt. Many were all too clear about their gifts. They did not have any! They had been schooled in the good British notion of underplaying every ability, and thinking that every eagerness to be involved in doing something showed either how ambitious or how vain they were. A number, especially of those not academically qualified, felt intimidated by the whole experience. Much affirmation needed to take place.

However we had made a start, and some signifi-cant achievements resulted. Certainly the whole idea of every-member ministry had been clearly established in people's minds. A good number of people were recruited into active service. Those we did get round to were helped, either into a ministry they had not previously been doing, or into feeling that the church recognised and affirmed what they were doing, or to believe that we did value them and that God could use them.

Since those days we have attempted the exercise in different ways, building on our experience. We have held a number of Ministry Sundays. Initially the intention was to use these to recruit new people into active service.

After we returned to the new St Thomas's we did a further large-scale exercise which Adele Fox, our parish worker, headed. It used some very fine graphics work based on the idea of a jigsaw, and on finding our place in the Lord's work. By this time we had leadership sufficiently established to widen greatly the number of people involved in the operation.

We now see recruiting, as we call it, a process in which a number of people are involved. The supporting fellowship group leaders have a crucial part to play in getting to know people and pointing them in the right direction. The leaders of our varied ministry teams need to be keeping those group leaders informed about needs that they have. Linking the two are ministry leaders in each congregation whose task it is to help forward the whole serving arm of the church's life.

Principles for Individuals

Out of these experiences of attempting to mobilise the whole membership, four elements in the service of each church member have been of great importance. All too often we fail to live by them, but they remain important guidelines for us.

1 Know your calling

I was sure that grace was the most effective, and fitting, basis for motivation. But how to help everyone to serve God out of a sense of calling rather than from moral duty, was a new skill to learn.

Our experience about giving during the building project was a great help here. We had learnt that the only safe way to help people know what to do was to encourage them to pray and ask God to show them. We were learning to do the same thing in ministry as well. When individuals were invited to take on some task they were urged to pray that God would make his will clear. If they did not sense his leading they were encouraged not to take on the task.

Appointing Chris Leach to head our children's work in 1986 was instructive in this way.

I went to one person and asked her to lead it, stating what I said earlier about it being all right to say no, if she did not feel called of God. She did not feel called, but had never before said no to meeting an evident need. It was a struggle for her, in which she needed my support and encouragement to break free and not take on this responsibility. It was a liberating experience. I rejoiced for her, and exercised faith for the children's work.

I then went to Chris Leach, and invited her. Chris was well able to decline, and did so speedily. However, I had evidently got this one right, as a few weeks later Chris came back to me to say she had had a dream in which she was in the centre of a large group of children, and she felt that God was saying the work with children was his call to her.

And so it has proved.

The cost of this approach has been letting go of control so that God could lead. It has often meant taking a step of faith by not putting pressure on someone to take on some vital role. Yet God has proved his faithfulness to us. It was a high risk policy, but it has borne a rich harvest of faith-filled service.

2 Do one job and do it well

We discovered early on that we had a core group who were doing many — undoubtedly too many — tasks, with an outer circle of people either content to leave it to others, or not feeling able to get in on the act. As part of our protection of the flock, we started to watch out for any ways that we were 'oppressing all our workers' (Isaiah 58.3). To some people we had to say, 'You are doing five jobs in the church. We really appreciate all that you are doing; but now can we talk about which four you need to hand over?'

One of the reasons for doing this was that we found that those who were doing many tasks tended not to be fully committed to any one of them. When you are doing a number of different ministries you can live with the fact that none is going well: the reason is that you do not have the time they need. However, when you are down to one, and it is still not working, you start to face why and seek answers from God.

We were surprised to discover that, contrary to popular opinion, it is not usually the church that over burdens such people, but the people them-selves. Many visits revealed those still seeking to earn their salvation by good works. There is a double tragedy in this approach. It does not earn salvation, and it diverts the glory from the grace of God to the nobility of the servant. It was this that Jesus was dealing with when he said of the Pharisees 'truly they have their reward'.

Over the years we have come to realise that some people have the time or energy or sheer ability to do more than one job, but we still seek to watch it, and I continue to be involved in visiting people to take jobs off them. We have certainly not achieved this fully, and continually lapse from this goal, but it is a yardstick by which to measure the best way for people to be working in the life of the church.

3 A time limit for every task

A further ground rule that emerged was to specify the length of time a job is to be done for. There are two particular advantages in this. First, it gives the church some continuity by reducing the frequency with which someone starts a ministry, loses interest, and moves on. We often give people (and the leaders they will be working with) a trial, or experimental, period in some task to see if that is what they should be doing. We are not wanting to trap people in a task that is really 'not them'. However, once that has been clarified we then agree how long it is to be exercised for. That gives us stable leadership and work within that activity.

It also gives the person a clear goal. We found this particularly helpful with the task of supporting fellowship leader. Part of that job is to help the group to grow and divide. If you take the task of leader on for an indefinite period then the matter of multiplying the group is something that can always be left until another time. If, however, you have three years to achieve that goal then the work is on right from the start.

While thinking over these things, two scriptures and one salutary experience clarified the whole issue. Jesus said, in his prayer in John 17.4, 'I have brought you glory on earth by completing the work that you gave me to do.' In similar vein the apostle Paul, speaking to the elders at Ephesus, said 'I consider my life worth nothing to me, if only I may finish the race and complete the task the Lord Jesus has given me' (Acts 20.24). I was struck by these because I knew not only that 'a woman's work is never done', but also that the same applies to vicars. There is always more to do, and that is true for the church and the Christian. Yet Jesus and Paul knew the limits of their responsibilities and were able to recognise when the job was done. It seemed right to give to God's people at St Thomas's the same job satisfaction: the sense of a task completed and a job well done.

This principle was powerfully driven home to me by the arrival of a new member in the church.

This man had been an active member of another church and eventually became the church secretary. After eight years he decided he wanted to give it up and so handed in his resignation. The church implored him to carry on: so he did. A year later he tried again, and — as the result of further moral pressure — agreed to stay on. After five more years of this, something in him snapped. He bundled up the books, put them in a plastic bag, and put them with a note of his resignation on the clergyman's doorstep. The next Sunday he turned up at St

Thomas's. He was very reluctant to be involved in any jobs.

We normally reckon on jobs being taken on for three years, though for some it is shorter, and for others (such as churchwarden) we look for a longer period. When the three years are up that does not mean that the person cannot continue. Rather it gives us as a church the opportunity to express thanks to the person for completing the task they have been given. Then we can sit down and talk about where they go next in ministry. It may be to continue for another three years — but that is separate from what they have done. That job is done, and we want them to enjoy that fact.

This does, of course, involve the leaders in exercising faith. Someone may have done a very good job, and yet feel it is right not to continue. We do not make their standing down conditional on finding someone to take over from them. The leaders have to exercise faith that either God does not want the work to continue, or that someone else will emerge. That is what happens time and time again.

4 Working in teams

Early in the days of the fellowship groups we had seen the value of working in a team. We found that individuals working on their own tended, when problems arose, to react by wondering what they had done wrong. However, put them to work with even one other person, and then, when problems arise, the usual reaction is likely to be to search for what can be done together to put things right.

There was a further reason for putting an

emphasis on teams. It meant that on-the-job training and support could be given. We could spot the particular gifts that individuals had, and find ways in which they needed help.

A further, and important, reason for teams is to maintain vision.

Vision fades so easily. A person can begin with such high hopes, and great expectations, but — in the cold light of day, and faced with the limitations imposed on us by having to work with people — that vision fades until it is simply a description of the achievable. Yet the kingdom is all about something happening that is of God, and is truly beyond us. We wanted to find ways of maintaining that vision, and the commitment in prayer that goes with it.

To this end we have developed a definition of a kingdom team:

> *A kingdom team is*
> *a group of believers,*
> *sharing a common vision*
> *who work and pray together*
> *in order to see God at work*
> *in and through and beyond*
> *their working together.*

Each phrase is important. In particular we found praying together and defining the vision are of primary importance. We want a vision that is not only clear, but beyond us in the sense that we are looking for the coming of God's kingdom and must expect his action.

Such teams are our goal. Some teams are a marvellous example of this, some settle for something much less, and others stagger on from crisis to crisis. Knowing what sort of team we want to create helps those in leadership to know where we are going. We certainly are not there, yet.

Principles for the Church

As our experience of serving God has grown we have learnt some important lessons about how best, as a church, to handle our participation in the mission of Jesus to the world around us.

First, we have taken a gifts-based ministry approach. By this I mean that the shape of the church's service is significantly shaped by the gifts and vision that individual members in the church have.

There are some activities which the church owns as an organisation, and is therefore committed to maintaining. Chief among these is our work with children on Sundays. There are also practical and administrative activities which we see as essential to our functioning at present. These include having a worship team, a team of stewards, and a team of people to operate the overhead projector and the amplification system. Obviously these needs might change. A complete staff team made up exclusively of operatic stars might make amplification redundant! Satellite television might enable us to beam the words of songs to every seat and thus dispense with overhead projector operators! For the present they are essential.

Before I arrived in Crookes, the church had already taken the step of handing over responsibility to the whole membership in the matter of giving to missionary work. I inherited a marvellous, and very simple, structure. Many churches allocate a specific amount of money out of their regular income to missionary work. It is sometimes a small amount ('all we can spare this year'); often it is a percentage (sometimes, in enlightened churches, it may be up to a tithe); usually it is both a struggle to find the money and a dilemma to know how much should be given.

St Thomas's had handed that decision back to the church by inviting everyone to specify how much of their giving was to go to the church, and how much to missionary work. The church in the fullest sense (that is the whole membership as a result of the sum of a host of individual decisions), makes that decision each year. It regularly results in one third of all the church's income being given away. The church has been handed back the responsibility and authority to make the decisions.

This gifts-based approach to ministry is a great stimulus to initiative. It saves new developments going through endless committees which sap the life out of an idea, causing it 'to die the death of a thousand qualifications'. It also avoids the church turning into a top-heavy bureaucracy.

Second, we have established a small team to oversee the church's ministry. They are called the Ministry Leaders. Their task is to oversee the whole shape and direction of the ministry which the church exercises both internally and externally, and they have authority delegated by the church council to apportion financial support and allocate room space to those groups that are wanting such help.

Principles for life

I have written exclusively so far about church activities or organisations. However, the mission of Christ is a much fuller work than can be contained simply through church activities. I see concentric circles, like a stone dropped into a pool, which express a series of ways in which that mission is being fulfilled by the people of God in today's world.

First, the coming of God's kingdom is expressed through the outworking and growth of Christian character, or Christ-likeness, in the people of God. A shop-keeper paid the church a compliment to Mary Mallon, wife of our present Baptist minister. 'Oh!' said the shopkeeper, 'you can tell St Thomas's people quite easily when they come in the shop.' Mary pressed for an explanation of how this was possible. 'Well,' came the reply, 'they have a peace and a sense of purpose in life that makes them different from others.' I am sure that is not always true of all of us all the time; but I rejoice that it shows. It is why we are in business.

Second, the character of Christ is expressed in the way we handle relationships. Two areas in particular are of great importance. First, is the way we handle our marriages. Christians not only have a high view of marriage, but also have a vital key to making them work. We know about forgiveness. Jay Adams in his book *Christian Living in the Home,* says 'The first thing and most important fact to remember about a truly Christian home is that sinners live there.' Although our marriages are not uniformly good, or always havens of peace, purity and pleasure, they do stand out as different. This has manifested itself in a very low divorce rate within the church. My estimate is that, in the seventeen years I have been at St Thomas's, we have had well over six hundred couples who for a greater or lesser time have been members of the church. To date I can recall less than six who, during their time as members of the church, came to the place of divorce. Each one was tragic, but the low level of divorce (lower than one in one hundred) is testimony to the grace of God.

The other area where the Christian approach to relationships works itself out is in attitudes to others at work. Here the seven or eight university lecturers in the congregation come immediately to mind. Typical of them is Terry Pratt (the churchwarden in the first half of the eighties). Terry has a marvellous, and highly appreciated, pastoral role within his department. Despite the fact that he is paid first to research and then to teach, he gives himself with immense care and understanding to help students in his department with problems and traumas that they face. It is not unknown for him to spend a whole day, when not lecturing, in such pastoral work. He then goes home and begins his work of lecture preparation. The love of Christ is being shed abroad through such care.

Third, the character of Christ is expressed in the way we use our resources of time, skills, and money. For a good number of church members there has been a conscious decision to move into, or not to move out of, the parish in order to be more available for service in the community. Many have made sacrifices in social life in order to give several evenings a week in the service of others through the church. For others a high level of giving has been their major contribution to the ministry of the church, enabling us to pay — for example — a full-time youth leader.

For some this availability to God has involved a willingness to forego paid employment in order to be more fully available for Christian service. One man, in his late forties, took early retirement so that he could exercise such a ministry. Others have much reduced their work involvement for the same reason. It has given us a small army of people who are available during the daytime for help with the counselling and healing ministry, and many other ministries. Of course, for the majority of people this would not be a right step. We certainly do not give any encouragement to the notion that church work is holier than other work. Being in the will of God is the only holiness any of us can know. Being a car mechanic under the bonnet of a car, and in the will of God, is a much holier work than praying in church when you should be under a bonnet.

Fourth, is the whole area of work, where the light of Christ is breaking in. From staff relationships in a school, the care of elderly clients by a hairdresser, or business ethics in the second-hand car trade, members of the church are not keeping their Christianity neatly boxed up in Sunday services, but are taking the risk of applying it to their everyday living.

Although we encourage everyone to be involved in some ministry in the life of the church, we do interpret that in a broad sense. It does not necessarily mean in a church activity. Rather, our definition of what and where the church is, controls how we see such Christian ministry. Some have felt the call of God to be deeply involved in the Sheffield refuge for battered wives. That is, at the organisational level, nothing to do with St Thomas's. At the deeper level, because they are part of the body of Christ in Crookes, the church is where they are. What is true for them is true for many others involved in similar ministries beyond the bounds of St Thomas's as an organisation. We seek to recognise this, and affirm and support such work in every way we can.

Three doctors in the congregation have felt the call of God to an inner-city practice which is at the sharp end of human suffering. They are seeing the victimised, the mentally sick, and the drop-outs of our society most of the time. Verbal and physical abuse goes with the job. They are there for no other reason than that they feel called of God to be. At present we are seeking to find ways in which a practical help and counselling service staffed by Christians from St Thomas's, and other churches, could be set up alongside them.

For some the call of God has taken them away from St Thomas's to become members of other, smaller, churches in the city. Others have heard God's call to full-time service at home and overseas. I am sure this fountain effect of the church's life is pleasing to God.

In these ways the mission of Christ and the ministry of the church are moving further and further out from the home base of the church. In so doing, and from the perspective of the kingdom of God, they are actually moving further and further into the mission field that Jesus entered. *Further out is further in*. Jesus first commissioned twelve followers, then more, and now us, to be involved in that mission with him. It is a costly, and risky place, taking us about beyond the safe harbour of the church onto the high seas of a suffering and hostile world. But it brings with it a joy that is unsurpassable; the cosmic joy of seeing sinners repent, bodies healed, lives made whole, and — in just a small way — society experiencing redemption.

Chapter Eight

AN ARRANGED MARRIAGE

When we returned to, and began to enjoy, the new St Thomas's we would have welcomed a period of rest. However, that was not to be. We already had one important matter waiting for our attention, and others were to follow swiftly. This first matter needing action was our relationship with Crookes Baptist church.

If ever there was an arranged marriage, this was it. Neither party, despite having been living in the same community for over eighty years, had any great awareness of the other. When put together by circumstances beyond their control neither had any notion that marriage would result. Survival was assumed to be the name of the game. No one saw beyond that.

This new chapter in the life of St Thomas's was another of those acts and gifts of God which have been such a feature of the church's life. God was planning what none of us had dreamed of. Our experience was to be an outworking in life of Paul's great passage on the unity of the church as recorded in Ephesians chapter four.

God's Gift

That chapter begins with a series of resounding
affirmations of the unity God has given to the
church.

> There is one body and one Spirit
> —just as you were called to one hope when you were
> called —
> one Lord, one faith, one baptism;
> one God and Father of all,
> who is over all and through all and in all!
> (Ephesians 4.4-6)

The emphasis and thrust of what Paul says is
expressed in the opening exhortation: 'Make every
effort to keep the unity of the Spirit in the bond of
peace' (Ephesians 4.3). Unity is not to be *achieved*,
but *received*. It is not a goal, but a gift. It is
sometimes said, 'You can choose your friends, but
you cannot choose your family.' Family is part of
the givenness of life. So it is in the family of God.
We were, in surprising ways, about to discover the
reality of this truth.

Coming Together

It was the disruption and distraction of the church
extension project which was the spark that miracu-
lously set such damp tinder, as two churches with
no plans for unity, alight.

When the architect first made it clear that we
would need to move out of our church building for
eighteen months or so our response was clear.
'Impossible: there is nowhere to go.' However, we
were continually saying 'impossible' throughout the

building project and then having to eat our words. After the initial, 'impossible' reaction we realised that we ought to research the situation. I asked Richard Laughlin, who by that time had come out of lecturing and was our full-time church administrator, to see if he could spy out any promised land. He came back with a good report of the local Baptist church. We knew little enough about Mulehouse Road Baptist Church, though we were aware that their congregation of forty or so did not always use their church building for worship. They also used the adjoining hall — endearingly called 'the school hut'.

Enquiries soon uncovered what the Prayer Book calls the 'prevenient' grace of God. The original meaning of the word prevent is 'to go ahead', preparing the way. Hence the well known Collect, 'Prevent us, O Lord, in all our doings with thy most gracious favour.' The meaning is much more positive than it sounds. That was what we were discovering. Unity was on his agenda, part of his plan for the two churches, and preparations had already been made.

First, the possibility of St Thomas's moving in was seen by the Baptists as good news, and the gift of God to be welcomed. Already they held their evening services in the school hut: forty people in a three-hundred-seater church is no way to build an intimate sense of the presence of God. They would gladly move the morning service (of similar size) out too, and make way for us. It suited their purposes as perfectly as it matched our needs.

Second, there were financial attractions. Like many small churches the Baptists were struggling to find the resources to maintain a building and a full-time minister. They had only recently, five years earlier, taken on a full-time minister after a period of twenty years without one. Although they had seen some growth, resources of money and manpower were fully stretched. The income from hiring the church to St Thomas's was to be a godsend: as was the availability of the building to us.

The homeless Anglicans and the penniless Baptists discovered each other as God's opportune gift to each other. Though the needs have changed the discovery still continues.

Third, one of the most striking evidences of God's plan for the two churches emerged when we came to talk about how our growing number of mid-week activities could possibly be accommodated within the restricted confines of the Mulehouse Road Baptist church site. Quite reasonably the Baptists said that, whenever they were not using the school hut during the week, it would be possible for us to use it. With some trepidation we sat down and looked at the diaries of both churches: most days we both had some committee, youth work, worship group, or other mid-week activity. To our amazement and relief the two programmes of the churches fitted like the teeth of cogwheels into each other. They meshed together perfectly, and required no changes to anyone's diary. No group or activity had to change time, let alone, as we had feared, to close down for eighteen months, 'or so'.

The fourth sign of the hand of God upon the coming together of the two churches was the spiritual unity we discovered together. So little had we had contact with each other that we were only dimly aware of the experience of renewal that both churches had been through in the 1970s. We found an immediate and exciting spiritual affinity, and knew a joy in prayer and work together which blessed both churches. What had been seen as a necessary task became a place to enjoy each other, and to discover God answering our prayers about the mass of practical details that resulted from ecclesiastical cohabitation.

The fifth way in which we experienced God's gift of unity was in the way we were able to relate together. We quickly found good relationships, built as much on mutual respect as on the sheer enjoyment of working together, to be a further sign of the kingdom coming among us. Yet even then none of us had any idea that this was for anything more than eighteen months, 'or so'!

Moving in

Most of us know the horrors, and decisions, of moving house after just five or ten years. Moving church after one hundred and forty years can hardly be imagined.

It was certainly hard work. The Anglicans, with our greater numerical strength, had offered to prepare for the greatly increased use of the school hut, by building cupboards, and a kitchen area, and by decorating and curtaining the building. It was all done speedily and to an impressive standard.

Our last Sunday at St Thomas's closed with a memorable valedictory service for our curate Patrick Coghlan, and his wife Gillian, who were about to leave for mission service in Salvador, Brazil. They were to work under the auspices of the South

American Missionary Society. The general secretary of SAMS had been due to speak, but he went down ill. The inspired substitute was Michael Cole, chairman of the SAMS Council, and my predecessor as vicar. It was the eighth anniversary, to the day, of his own farewell service at the end of his time in Crookes. For Patrick, Gill, and the whole church this was a commissioning for God's call into the unknown.

Then came the never-to-be-forgotten week of moving in. It proved to be the first week of a severe winter, made worse by a disastrous combination of thaw and freeze which left the whole of Crookes (itself four hundred feet above sea level) a veritable skating rink. To complicate matters, the gritting lorries were strike-bound throughout the week.

Every night, as part of a highly organised plan of military-like precision, an army of people arrived at Mulehouse Road to clear and clean, to create, and in particular to carry, a vast amount of material. It is amazing how heavy, and greedy for space, are smaller items like prayer books, hymn books, and Bibles, when they come in lots of four hundred. For me the highlight, and greatest cause for concern, was the moving of six pianos across the increasingly glistening sheet of ice that we were daily polishing. I knew it was fitting that the cherubim and seraphim fall down before the glassy sea; but our prayer that we would not follow their example was duly answered. We moved, by the grace of God, without accident, injury, or loss.

Together

Our stay of ninety-nine Sundays was a memorable

time. We frequently reflected on the experience of the children of Israel and their wilderness wanderings. Out of deference to our Baptist hosts we sought not to lay stress on the notions of the barren, hostile, and above all waterless, place through which the children of Israel had passed.

In fact it was warm, and welcoming. Sometimes too much so, as when one of our Anglican clergy, John Foote, walked into the minute vestry and went straight through the floor boards, up to his knees, due to the dry rot he had uncovered. By then we knew we were right in!

Interestingly we discovered that worshipping in a smaller building, with a much lower ceiling, aided the sense of intimacy, informality, and fellowship. Although in a strange building, we immediately felt very much together. Indeed, half-way through our stay we had to make adjustments because we realised that the intimacy with one another actually tipped the scale away from a sense of the presence and majesty of God. Adjustments of a different kind were needed when we returned to the new St Thomas's with what felt like its vast acres of open space.

We were together in the same building yet, in so many ways, that was far from what we were. Both congregations were worshipping in unfamiliar surroundings. Both were focused on finding and preserving their identity in a changed environment. Neither still had any idea of the way that lay before us.

Diversity

In his passage on the unity of the church in

Ephesians, Paul, having laid the foundation of that unity, immediately goes on to develop the theme of the rich diversity of gifts that the ascended Lord has given to the church. In Romans 12 the focus is on the serving gifts, and in 1 Corinthians 12 and 14 it is on the supernatural gifts. Here Paul writes about the church-building gifts. The sheer variety is as important as the specific details of each gift. Having been brought together in the purposes of God we were about to discover something of the rich tapestry of the church as God intends it to be.

Humanly speaking the idea of a longer-term and closer working together arose out of a chance remark I made, at a local ministers' fraternal, to the Baptist minister, David Morrell. He had been expressing some of the frustrations of having to put so much time and energy into sustaining the fabric of the church building. Without realising the implications, I had said, 'You would be better off coming back (to the new St Thomas's) with us.' It was evidently an idea whose time had come. No sooner had it been expressed than it took root, spread rapidly, and in due course became very fruitful. How this might happen was totally uncharted territory for all of us. So began a process of exploring the new world of local ecumenical projects.

Local Ecumenical Projects

We quickly discovered the basic shape. A local ecumenical project (an LEP) is the legal means that the member churches of the British Council of Churches have established to enable two or more denominations to work together. It can vary from simply two or more churches using the same building, but in all other respects having a separate life of their own, to two or more churches aiming to be as fully integrated as possible: in fact seeking to be one church. That was our goal.

Three documents are produced in the setting up of an LEP to which we decided to add our own fourth. First is the declaration of intent: this spells out the aim. Second is what is called a shared building agreement. This is a technical and legal document which in essence enables a Baptist church to function in what legally remains an Anglican building. Third, and really the most vital part, is the constitution, which spells out details such as the forms of service to be used, how the two churches will govern themselves, how baptism will be handled, and other matters. We were advised not to tie the hands of future generations by making this document too full and detailed. We kept it as brief as possible, and for this reason felt that there would be value in filling out its meaning in a commentary on the constitution which was the fourth document, and the one we added. It was certainly not our intention to hide anything from anyone and so we decided that this was the best way to explain the intention behind some of the general statements of the constitution, without those details becoming in any way binding.

Negotiations

We made a first attempt at working out how a united church might operate in late 1979 and on into the new year. We soon discovered, however, that the pressure of the final year of the building project made taking on another major venture impossible. We found the Baptists understandably pressing for decisions which we were not able to give the time, attention, or emotional energy to resolving. We agreed to delay any further discus-sion until we had moved back and settled in. It would have been good to have gone back together, but it was just not possible. We were touching on an important part of our diversity: naturally the two congregations had very different pressures and time-scales. We were beginning to listen to, and to respect, that diversity and to find ways to work with it — rather than against each other.

It was into the autumn of 1981, two years later, before we were able to begin again. During this time the LEP became, unitedly, our first priority, and events moved swiftly.

There were three phases in the process of negotiations. The first lasted just one meeting but was a crucial part. We began by each sharing our own experience of God, and his hand upon our lives, and our membership of the Christian church. Immediately we stumbled upon the ironies of our Christian nurture. Though an Anglican clergyman, I had in fact not been baptised as an infant. Only after coming to faith as a teenager was I baptised, as a believer, even if with what some would feel was an inadequate amount of water. The Baptist minister, David Dewey (David Morrell having left for a church in Birmingham a year previously) had in fact been brought to faith and nurtured as a young believer in an Anglican church.

We were going to be a crazy mixed-up church!

Indeed one of the important things that emerged from this phase of personal testimony and introduction was a sobering fact. Only one of the seven of us had consciously chosen the denomination we were now in. For six of us we acknowledged that, humanly speaking, it was an accident of history (where we had been brought up, and been taken to church), or of geography (where the nearest church was) that had dictated where we worshipped. Our denominational convictions *followed on from* that prior decision. It was a sobering realisation and alerted us to the danger of over-emphasis of denominational convictions — deeply held and embedded in us as people though they were.

The seventh member of the group, Steve, had a story which was full of irony in our situation. As a student he had become a member of St Thomas's. He was happily involved with us until one Sunday when I preached a sermon on infant baptism. It was then that he realised he was a Baptist by conviction, and did the honourable thing of leaving to join Crookes Baptist Church. Here he was now talking about how to rejoin.

The second phase of the negotiations involved the greater part of our monthly Thursday evening, and Saturday morning, meetings. They took the form of presentations from both sides on a series of major issues: usually including a brief paper presenting the convictions of the Anglican or Baptist church on a particular subject. Topics included church government, worship, leadership, evangelism, and baptism. Out of this six-month process one over-riding fact emerged. It was this: apart from the matter of baptism, we discovered that we had no theological disagreements. Time and time again we saw that what the other church was saying was not in conflict with what we believed, but rather an enriching balance and complement to what we held to be important. We ended up wondering how our two churches had ever fallen out.

Sadly the cause in history lay largely with the Anglican persecution of Baptists, some even being put to death by drowning, which was judged to be the appropriate punishment for people teaching such heresy. It has led me to the conclusion that the way forward in church unity is by going backwards in repentance. Not until we Anglicans repent of our treatment of Wesley will that division be healed; nor will the larger divide between catholics and protestants be overcome until the Roman Catholic church repents of its treatment of Luther and the reformers.

When we discussed public worship, we Anglicans explained why liturgy and form and order were valued in our church. The Baptists then explained why freedom, spontaneity, and participation were important for them. However these did not exclude but, rather, balanced each other. We Anglicans said that we did value liturgy, but that we had been incorporating spontaneity and participation already and were eager to learn more. The Baptists were saying that though they valued freedom they were certainly aware of the value of giving more shape and order to their worship.

Again, when we talked about church government and leadership, we discovered the possibility of a richer diversity and strength if we were together. 'Yes, we do believe,' said the Anglicans, 'in a proper ultimate pastoral authority for the leader in a local church; but we have also discovered (not least through our building project) the importance of the whole church participating in the discernment of, and decisions about, the major directions of the life of the church.' 'We think we have some record of whole-church decision making,' said the Baptists, 'but we certainly want to avoid an unbiblical form of church democracy, and want to give the leaders the freedom and authority to lead.'

This was the heart of our discovery.

It felt as if we were putting back together two halves of a valuable, but fragile, work of art that had somehow been tragically broken. We held to the truths that our forefathers in the faith had fought for: indeed some had died for those truths, like justification by faith, believer's baptism, the authority of scripture, and the freedom of the conscience of the individual. We were convicted of the prejudices that had grown up over this divide, in which we had participated. The absence of relationship between the members of our two churches had fed that division and opposition. Now, by a process of listening, and learning, we came to value not only each other (phase one of the negotiations), but also each other's convictions and traditions (phase two of the negotiations). Like the old Guinness advert we realised we had been guilty of the attitude 'I don't like it because I've never tried it'!

The third step flowed naturally out of the latter position. We wanted to find how we could put these two parts of the divided body of Christ back together. This involved drawing up a constitution and writing a commentary on it so that the members of both churches could themselves decide if this was of God and the way that we should be going.

The Decision

The negotiations were completed early in 1982. The next stage was to go to the membership of both churches to seek their discernment of what had been done and, hopefully, to gain their approval.

For the Anglicans there were substantial changes required. The church had been growing steadily for over fifteen years, and had just been through the demanding church extension project. We were looking for a quieter and more settled period, not for changing the very nature of the church we were. There was also a feeling of not wanting to change a winning team. Indeed some of the officials in the diocese expressed amazement at what we were contemplating. 'Having spent all that money on your building are you now going to give it away?' was one remark made to me. It was not a particularly enlightened attitude but did express the fear that we might somehow be giving away something vital. Some, however, caught the vision and were eager; others trusted the leaders and were willing; a few simply accepted what seemed inevitable.

For the Baptists, the decision would be even more far-reaching. Pulling back from establishing the LEP would immediately immerse them in the old struggle for survival. Going forward into the LEP seemed a dangerous journey into the unknown. What could be known was no less threatening. It would involve leaving the Mulehouse Road site. It would almost certainly involve the demolition of their church building. It would result in their being part of both a large, and a predominantly Anglican, church; where they had been a small and unmistakably Baptist church. For a few their Baptist convictions could not countenance the compromise of being associated with a church that practised infant baptism (however disciplined that practice might be). For some the upheaval and change was more than they could cope with. However, the great majority were convinced.

The vote was taken on the same night in both churches — so that we would not be influenced by how each other voted. We arranged runners between the two meetings in order that, in each church, after the result of the vote was announced, the vote of the other church could be announced too. The Anglican vote was held as the focal point of the (April) annual general meeting in 1982. Over two hundred people had gathered. The arguments had already been rehearsed so we simply held the vote. The voting was decisive. For, 200; against, five. A majority of over ninety-seven per cent. The Baptist vote was a clear yes, even if not so overwhelming. Seventeen of the twenty-one people present voted in favour: a majority of over eighty per cent.

By the October of that year, the LEP was inaugurated, and henceforth St Thomas's would be an Anglican and Baptist church.

Harmony

Paul's great exposition of the nature of the church (in Ephesians 4) moves from unity, through diversity, on to harmony: the blessing and maturity that come from holding diversity in unity.

> Speaking the truth in love, we will in all things grow up into him who is the Head, that is Christ.

> From him the whole body, joined and held together
> by every supporting ligament, grows and builds
> itself up in love, as each part does it work.
> (Ephesians 4.15,16)

How this has happened, in so far as it has, is the
final part of the story. It is over six years since the
establishing of the LEP, and we can look back on
solid achievement, as well as significant testing of
the united church that had been established.

Working it out

The first question most people ask on hearing of a
united Anglican/Baptist church (which seems such
a contradiction in terms) is, 'What do you do about
baptism?' It is an obvious point.

It is important to recognise that the foundation of
our solution to this problem is mutual respect for
each other's tradition: not simply because it is
tradition, but because the two forms of handling
baptism grow out of sincerely held understandings
of what the scriptures say. The problems are
primarily over the Anglican practice of infant
baptism, although there are aspects of the Baptist
approach which appear defective to Anglicans.
However, freedom of conscience was one of the
foundational concerns of the original Anabaptists:
and this they sought not just for themselves but for
others too. Without this mutual respect and the
giving of freedom to others to follow their conscience the LEP could not stand.

One rule that emerged out of this was an
agreement not to proselytise. Obviously, everyone
is free to express their opinion but, especially
among the leaders, it is important to direct those

making decisions to go and talk to someone from the other church, as well as to present both sides of the case as fully as one can. Our agreement was to allow freedom of conscience and to practise both patterns of initiation alongside each other. We have found, in practice, that at any one service it is better not to mix the two together (a Baptist dedication and an Anglican infant baptism are best separated); but within the one church members of each denomination follow their own church's initiation pattern.

One of the first practical steps was to build a baptistry into the worship area: on the dais under the communion table. That was part of the commitment in establishing the LEP. As Anglicans that presented no problems: we have been glad to have a baptistry. Practically every year we have had adult baptisms within our confirmation service. Not that we have an 'ours' and 'yours' approach to such baptisms. One of our recent, and very effective, evangelistic services included seven believers' baptisms. Obviously the whole church, not just Baptists, took part in inviting people to that service.

As far as Anglicans wanting, after infant baptism, to be baptised as believers by total immersion is concerned we have inevitably had our struggles, but the rules are clear.

Those rules were established at the outset in consultation with the South Yorkshire sponsoring group under whose authority the LEP was set up. It represented the two denominations and had final authority in what was allowed.

The rules were quite specific on this point. Someone baptised as an infant, but now convinced of the rightness of believer's baptism, can (if they

have not been confirmed) be baptised as believers.
They then become Baptists within the LEP. The
reason that confirmation is the test is because some
objective rule, rather than subjective decision
(such as it being thought pastorally appropriate),
makes for much less difficulty. Confirmation, being
a public acknowledgement of the validity of baptismal vows taken on by others on our behalf in
infancy, is the appropriate point of no return.
Those who have been confirmed, who cannot
accept the renewal of baptismal vows as sufficient,
and (as the Prayer Book puts it) 'cannot quiet their
conscience', cannot therefore be baptised within
the LEP. Some, not many, have felt the need to go
elsewhere to receive such baptism. We have found
it helpful to see this as a purely Anglican pastoral
problem, and not to muddle the LEP with such
matters. With a few hiccups, it has worked well.

Worship

We had agreed to handle worship 'with the Anglican form, and the Baptist style'. We started with a
monthly Baptist communion service on the first
Sunday of each month. More recently the frequency has been increased to one Baptist service a
month at each service time (we now have four
services on a Sunday). This proposal came from the
Anglican clergy during the time between two
Baptist ministers, which suggests that the LEP was
working well.

There has never been any evidence to suggest
that regular worshippers opt for the services of a
particular denomination with the LEP. Exactly the
same people, in the same numbers, can be expected

for a Baptist communion service on the first Sunday of the month as can be expected two weeks later for the Anglican communion. The services are seen as St Thomas's worshipping together. All services are part of 'our' worship.

Apart from one service a month communion is administered in the seats rather than at the rail. Although this is usual Baptist practice the Anglicans had been following this pattern prior to the forming of the LEP. It enables us to administer to four hundred people in six or seven minutes in a quiet and unhurried way which underlines the corporate nature of communion. When asked whether we use the one cup of the Anglicans or the many individual cups of the Baptists, I find it difficult to know how to put the answer. We actually use fourteen. The cup and plate are passed along the rows of seats. I suppose you could describe it as a 'semi-individual multiple-one-cup' means of administration!

Virtually all our continued struggles about how to handle worship are the problems of a large church, rather than of an LEP. We have to watch attaching Anglican or Baptist labels to problems, the vast majority of which would be exactly the same if we were a large Anglican or a large Baptist church.

Church Government

Although we did not put it, or think of it, in these terms at the outset we have really handled church government on the same principle as worship — using the Anglican form, and the Baptist style.

The Anglican form is used in that we have a

church council which makes decisions on behalf of
the congregation. It is elected by all those on the
Anglican electoral roll, and all those on the Baptist
register. Any of these can stand for election.

The Baptist style has become increasingly important as the church has grown in size. Paddy Mallon,
who replaced David Dewey as Baptist minister
early in 1988, described the way the church works
as 'an ideal Baptist pattern'. The church council
functions as a management group responsible for
the many decisions about fabric, finance, and
worship that we continually face. The staff team
gives pastoral and spiritual leadership; with the
wardens functioning as advisers and supervisors.
All of the above is set in the context of a listening
style of leadership. Though we do not have a
church meeting or voting as such (something that in
any case Baptists consider a degenerate form of the
biblical principle of congregation decision-making)
a constant process of communication is going on
between the leadership and membership. It is a
two-way process by which vision and direction are
discovered, sharpened, and finally embraced and
acted upon.

This two-way communication is achieved in a
number of ways. We have used congregational
surveys from time to time. The preaching ministry,
the church newsheet, *Family Life,* and monthly
central prayer meeting (attended by up to three
hundred people) all play a crucial part. Regular
meetings with the leaders of fellowship and discipleship groups, and the use of specially prepared
study material, complete with group response
forms, also help. The whole process is set in the
context of a network of relationships in which ideas

flow both ways.

Just Testing

If I ended the story at this point the reader could be forgiven for thinking that, after the LEP was established, 'they all lived happily ever after'. That would not be true. We had seen the process in terms of courtship, engagement, and marriage. We were to discover that handling marital conflict continued the experience. The problems we have had have been valuable growth points. It has only been by working hard at 'speaking the truth in love' that we have found God's way of growing up into maturity in Christ: a process that is by no means complete. These struggles have been part of God's refining process for us as individual believers, for all those involved in leadership, and for the LEP itself, which has been tried, tested, purified, and (in the final issue) strengthened by what we have had to face.

First, we have seen the need to pass on the vision to the next generation of church members. The LEP came to birth out of relationships of mutual trust formed by working together. We had assumed that this is how it would continue, but assumptions have a habit of disappointing, and the next generation of church members need to be fired by the same vision. After just six years, it may well be too early to know if this is happening.

Second, we did survive what felt like a hijack attempt which was uncomfortable at the time. A small group who had evidently not 'bought into the vision' of respecting each other's views and working together in a mixed-denominational church, took up membership of the Baptist church within the LEP. Without the balance of the full Baptist tradition (not least, its concern for liberty of conscience for others) an attempt was made to push re-baptism. A campaigning mentality was let loose. By standing firm with this group we unearthed an underlying dissatisfaction among them with much that St Thomas's stood for. The bubble burst, and the group dispersed to other churches; though, significantly, practically none to Baptist churches. We were able to maintain good relationships for much of this period and to this day. The church, as well as the mercy, of God 'is much wider than the measure of man's mind' as the hymn writer put it. The vast majority of the church members were quite unaware that this was going on, and the whole episode was soon over, but not before much trauma and heartache had been experienced, particularly by the wardens and myself.

Third, has been a cluster of problems related to denominationalism. Being in the evangelical and charismatic traditions, both churches in the LEP put a clear emphasis on the priority of becoming, and living as, a Christian above any importance in being an Anglican or Baptist. However, the unintentional result is that the members are disinterested in, and even disown, anything to do with denominations. 'I am a Christian and I am not interested in belonging to any denomination' is a frequent and understandable, but dangerous, attitude. A consequence of this is to breed what I call a 'supermarket approach to Christianity'. This involves picking and choosing the parts we like out of both: typically, in our situation, an Anglican wedding followed by a Baptist dedication of the resulting offspring.

This is further complicated by our being a large church because it can, as it grows, function more and more like a denomination itself, providing a wealth of resources and contacts. Instead of creating a united Anglican and Baptist church we realised that we were in danger of aggravating Christian unity by creating a new denomination: a generation that is neither Anglican nor Baptist. 'Bapticans' perhaps!

We have responded to this problem in two ways.

While committed to the fact that 98% of our job is to help people to become and live as Christians, we also now include an element of conscious denominational emphasis. We are, after all, committed to the renewal of our two denominations. While seeking the grace of God to overcome denominational prejudices, we thank him for the riches of the faith preserved for us by our two denominational heritages. We want, like our fore-fathers, to pass on that faith to the next generation. We believe that the Holy Spirit has been active in those denominations down the centuries. We do not think that church history can be ignored, and its harsh lessons avoided. In an increasingly rootless society we believe that our two traditions give vital roots for the long-term health of the individual believer, and for the local church.

To this end the believer's baptism and the confirmation preparation courses now have a greater emphasis on denominational roots than they did when we were separate churches. We are not in the business of denying or neglecting our heritage from the past.

Moreover we have sought to encourage participation in denominational events and structures. Two major denominational events that have taken place in recent years at St Thomas's well illustrate this point. The first was a deanery agape — communion in the context of a three-course meal. The Baptists participated fully, as well as giving a disproportionately large amount of help in the preparations. The other was the whole day celebration, including this time a sit-down meal for four hundred people, to mark the two-hundredth anniversary of the foundation of the Yorkshire Baptist Association (which is nearly three times older than the Anglican diocese of Sheffield). This time it was only because of the large number of Anglicans helping that such an event was possible.

So our response to this continuing problem is a conscious choice to affirm, value, and teach about the roots of our two denominations. It is all part of our holding together in truth as well as in love.

Chapter Nine

HOLDING TOGETHER

Intention is easier than action. To agree to be united, whatever the difficulties faced, is easier than being united. Indeed we discovered that the South Yorkshire sponsoring group that had authorised the LEP was far from happy about our use of the word 'united'. They argued that the past completed tense is a dangerous one to use. Unity is fragile and cannot be assumed as something we once did. How right they were. Not that St Thomas's was a stranger to the problem of living together in love as a Christian community. As with most churches, we had had our fair share of strains; but through them God had graciously led us to points of reconciliation and deeper unity.

Built into the fabric of St Thomas's was the social conflict which marks so much of English culture. The church had been born out of that divide. In 1836 the labouring community had decided to build a Methodist chapel in the area. When the few wealthy 'church' people, living on the fringes of Crookes, discovered this they decided that a proper (that is, an Anglican!) church should be put up — fast. The race was on. I am glad to say that the Methodists won.

When I arrived in Crookes some of the older inhabitants told of the days at the end of the last century when the people of the community would turn out to see the wealthy going to church in their carriages. Today there is tension over the parking of cars in the crowded streets around the church. The social tensions from the past, though more complex and varied, are still with us today.

Other areas of conflict have already been mentioned, such as the death of many cherished activities, and the changes in the forms, times, and style and feel of our worship. The charismatic issue had added further conflict, and the building project, by its sheer size, and through the upheaval of moving churches, had added to the stress that was experienced. A member of the church summed it up so well when, during the building project, he sent me a postcard encouraging me in my leading of the church. In large letters on the front of the card, against a green background, were the words:

Constant change is here to stay

I pinned it up in my office for several years until I decided that change itself required that it did not stay for ever.

Out of these experiences, and the challenge of making unity between two denominations a reality, rather than an idea, seven lessons have been learnt about how to maintain the unity that the Spirit gives.

1 Keep Talking

This is perhaps a surprising place to begin, but we

found it one of the most vital ingredients of love. The story has already been told of how, through the supporting fellowships, the church was saved from major division through the personal relationships that crossed the potential charismatic divide.

Whenever hurt and conflict surface the temptation is to withdraw from others, lick our wounds, and to seek the company of like-minded people who will reinforce our judgement of others. The cross calls us to the vulnerable place where conflict is faced and handled. We have found that the existence of conflict does not of itself dishonour God. Rather, the way the church handles such conflict can demonstrate the power of the gospel to overcome the divisions of the world.

This is a costly way that involves openness, and a willingness to forgive the hurtful things that are said and done. It involves dying to self, and (especially in leadership) being willing to be a scapegoat for others.

2 Keep Moving

Although the sheer pace and speed of change had been a strain on the church, we had also seen how a definite purpose can be a powerful uniting force. Having a clear sense of direction had certainly brought unity to the church during the building project.

I love the story of the two ministers, of different denominations, who spent a morning together. At the end of their friendly exchanges one of them said to the other 'Ah well, brother, I suppose we must be getting back to the Lord's work: you doing it in *your* way and me doing it in *his!*' It sounds very arrogant, but the fact remains that discovering God's way is a great aid to unity. Rather than facing each other in conflict about which of us will win, the church needs to be side by side on its knees seeking to discover God's will, however costly that may be.

Sharing a common vision is usually the result of prayer. A church may focus on its leader or its vision. The more they overlap the better. However, it is much safer to focus on the vision of where we are going — rather than on who is leading us. The vision is likely to be larger, and stay longer. Our experience has been that while we were a church of under two hundred members it was possible for the church to unite around their relationship with the leader. Once that barrier of two hundred members is broken, the vision and direction of the church becomes the more important factor in its unity. A sign of health and life in a church is a shared sense of God's call, in a specific way, upon our life together. In a large church where nobody can know everyone it seems to me to be an essential unifying factor.

This is what I mean by keeping moving. If we can see together the direction in which God is taking us, we are much more likely to be 'of one heart and mind'. By contrast a directionless church is likely to be a divided church. The picture that comes to my mind at this point is of a flotilla of small boats crowded together for safety in the harbour. There is safety there, but it is also the place where they are most likely to bump and jostle each other. Once get them out on the high seas and they form a fleet going in the same direction and helping each other to get there.

Michael Ramsey, a former Archbishop of Can-

terbury, in speaking about unity said that the more
fully the church enters the world on the mission of
Jesus of Nazareth the more quickly will it find its
unity as a by-product of that activity.

To this end we have learnt how vital is the quality
and reality of our worship. As we put God first, and
listen to him, we find the unity (and forgiveness) he
wants to give his church. 'A church that prays
together stays together.'

3 Keep Listening

What I have said so far may sound like one-way
traffic: the church catching the vision of the leader
and leadership. That is important; but so is the
reverse — the leadership catching the church's
vision. This is where we have found listening to be
such a vital means of holding the church together in
unity.

Francis MacNutt says of prayer for healing that
you need to keep one ear open to God, and one to
the person for whom you are praying. The same is
true in healing the wounds within the body of
Christ. This involves an open style of leadership,
which is a high-risk policy, especially in a culture
that has exalted control as its primary value.
Openness and trust involve risk, and vulnerability.
It involves listening to, rather than taking up arms
against, our critics. They usually have a truth,
however hostile their presentation may on occasions be. Several elements of this listening process
have stood out for me over the years. Here are
some of my ground rules.

Don't take ideas personally. Leaders especially
become very protective of their ideas (we use the

tell-tale phrase 'it's his brain-child'). That is only one step removed from the fatal mistake of taking criticisms of ideas as an attack upon oneself. They are not. The other side of this is to take somebody else's ideas as a threat to our leadership. How wise Moses was to take to heart the management advice of his (non-believing) father-in-law, Jethro. How important it was for James not to be opposed to the taking of the gospel to the Gentiles just because other leaders, including that upstart Paul, were in on the action in a way he was not.

Let ideas out. We can be so protective of ideas that they have no chance to grow or mature. They need weathering. Good ideas, and more particularly God-ideas, can stand hammering: the truth will out. In fact I find this one of the best ways to test the rightness of new ventures — let the idea out· give people permission and encouragement to talk about it. If it is of God then conviction and support will grow. Moreover, in the process, the idea will be refined, matured and strengthened. It will benefit from the airing. If it is not of God it will fade and shrink like a burst balloon. How good it is to know that before we all jump on board.

Welcome conflict. What! Is this how to develop unity? Yes. 'Iron sharpens iron,' says Proverbs. Sir John Harvey-Jones, the former head of ICI, in his book *Making it happen,* says: 'In industry the optimum level of conflict is not zero,' adding that if the right decisions are to be taken it is essential that conflicting views are heard and thrashed out. We need a process of discussion and interaction to mature our thinking.

Wait for consensus. This is where timing is so important. We have on several occasions taken a vote at a church council meeting that was carried with only one or two against. We do not usually go ahead if it is a major new development. Just one person stood out against the final vote on developing congregations. I proposed we did not go ahead but called an additional council meeting to talk further. I spent a couple of hours with that person, a respected leader in the church, thrashing the whole issue out with him. The idea was significantly sharpened, he was convinced — and proposed the motion at the next meeting — and unity was not just maintained, it was strengthened. All too often we get into fight situations on such occasions and take as ammunition all those destructive weapons in our verbal armoury: 'you're against me', 'I take this personally', 'you are siding with the enemy'. All because patience, faith and listening are lacking. I should add that this has not led me to expect, or always wait for, a unanimous vote. I have too sober a view of human nature for that.

Incorporate their vision. As I have said, it does not matter where the ideas came from; what matters is our discerning whether they are part of God's plans. Moreover, because the members are the body of Christ, then surely our starting point is that their vision is part of God's call. Not always, but usually, is how I have seen it work out. This is the whole point of teamwork, which is what the church is. Everyone has a piece to contribute to the jigsaw of God's plan.

Yet when all this is said there is another side to the role of leader.

Resisting the pressure of private agendas from wrong, misguided and bad ideas is part of the role of a shepherd and protector of the flock. Here we have to make judgements, praying for the gift of discernment as we do so. There will always be people who want to hijack the church with their pet ideas. The church needs protection from them.

The Bishop of Sheffield, David Lunn, has paid St Thomas's the compliment (at least that is how I take it) of saying that what surprised him about the church is that 'there is no opposition'. In his experience this is unusual in the life of a church. My understanding is that the emphasis on listening and whole-church participation in discerning the vision is an important reason. Not that we are always all agreed; I, for one, do not always like what goes on. However, it makes a lot of difference if you feel you have been heard. None of us expects, or even wants, our way all the time, but we do need to feel we have been heard.

Listening then is a key to unity, and there is no more creative or unifying listening in a church than listening to God. What matters is not whether the ideas came from the minister or the cleaner, but whether it is of God. Hence, the vital importance of coming before God in prayer as a church.

4 Face Feelings

How powerful, for good or evil, are our emotions. Yet the Christian church often functions as though they did not exist, or could safely be ignored. The fact is that they cannot be ignored. Rather, if we can harness them they can be a great force for good in the work of God.

Where there is conflict, tension, misunderstanding, or plain disagreement, we can benefit enormously by looking below the surface and seeing what emotional currents are flowing. Behind practically all ideas, and certainly behind all arguments for, or against, there are feelings. They form the hidden agenda: very often that agenda is the real one, which is why we need to understand it. The fear, anxiety or sense of threat surfaces first; and then come the theological arguments. To pay attention to the theology alone is to miss the best part of the argument.

One of the liberating results for me, of listening to the emotions in a situation, has been that once I have seen what is happening emotionally in a conflict situation (in me as well as in others) I am then both free to discover how to deal with the emotions, and also not bound to be controlled by them. Our experience has been that when God is calling us to let go of something we have been doing, or to begin a new phase, there is a great value in considering how people will feel. Without changing what we are going to do, we can harness enthusiasm, answer the doubts, pay attention to the hopes, comfort the sense of loss, and do whatever is needed to deal with those feelings.

As with financial resources so with emotional ones, we have learnt first to discern what God is calling us to do, then to look at what our resources are, and finally to trust God to fulfil our resources rather than diminish his plans. A church, faced with a building/financial need, can simply say, 'How much have we got?' and build accordingly. Inevitably it will be a monument to unbelief. The better course is to ask, 'How much do we need?' and then

pray and give to see that met. So too at the
emotional level. When change is required we do
not ask, 'How much change will people accept?',
but 'What help will be needed — at the emotional
level — to bring about this change?'

I stumbled across this, in the mid 1970s, when we
abandoned our annual garden party. For just a few
it was a painful experience. The garden party had
become the focal point of their church life. Painful
though it was, the loving action was to uncover that
undue emphasis, not pander to it. For many there
was a sense of loss at the passing of a very enjoyable
social event as we all worked together to create an
interesting day. That was a valid point, and we
listened to those feelings and kept our eyes open for
a replacement for that loss. The building project
included a vast heightening of that sense of working
together to create something important.

I have come to see, particularly in a church where
there is much change, that that sense of loss and
bereavement needs to be recognised; not least
when we stop something good. I was so grateful to
the wardens for alerting the staff team when, in
September 1987, we divided the morning service
(10.30am) into two services (9.15am and 11.15am).
Everyone's eyes were on the challenge and potential of the change. It was the wardens who got us, at
the last 10.30am service, to take time to thank God
for the past — and to let go. We were not scrapping
something bad, but letting go of something that had
had an enormous effect for good in the life of the
church. It was important to give that recognition,
and to let go with thanksgiving. Those eager for,
and those hesitant about, the coming changes were
united in that act.

5 Give Headroom

By 'giving headroom', I mean allowing people to express their ideas, and the opportunity to act when they sense any call of God (however tentative), and the freedom and authority to follow their calling. In this way we can avoid having frustrated passengers.

I will return to this later, but our goal has been to find structures that enable people to be active in their service of God. Our attitude has been 'Let a thousand flowers bloom, and you will be surprised how little room for weeds is left!' This has been a significant aid to having a happy, and consequently united, church. Not that we achieve this all the time; or always know which flowers need watering with our limited resources of money and manpower.

6 Recognise the Spiritual Dimension

It was Archbishop William Temple who said 'I believe in one holy catholic and apostolic church ... and bitterly regret that it nowhere exists!' Such is the impact that the devil has had upon the 'seamless robe of Christ', his church. Satan's efforts find focus so often in creating distrust, division and disunity. We need to be on our guard. We also need to know how to use the weapons at our disposal. Overcoming evil with good; not retaliating when individuals are touched on a raw nerve and blow their top.

'Hyping' the atmosphere is one of the tactics of the enemy. Chris Bonnington, the mountaineer, has said that the only person he would risk taking up Mount Everest was a person who 'goes calm in a crisis'. Cooling the temperature is a vital preliminary to dealing with conflict.

It is often a costly path, functioning like blotting paper, or a punch bag, but in Jesus we have the supreme model of overcoming evil with good: 'who when he was reviled did not revile in return, but committed his cause to him who judges justly' (1 Peter 2.23).

Prayer, love and honest searching of our own heart for any causes of hurt and division in us are weapons that God has given us to win in such spiritual battle.

7 Letting Go

Battles, conflicts, and divisions do happen in the best regulated families and the finest churches. So they are bound to happen in ours. At St Thomas's we have been no exception. Some left because we became charismatic; others left because we were not being charismatic enough and wanted to establish their own church. Within a matter of days two people left, one because St Thomas's was becoming 'just a church for the local community'; the other left because St Thomas's was 'no longer a church of the local community'. You certainly cannot please all the people all the time. The greatest danger lies in attempting to do so.

I have come to the conclusion that those of us in leadership have, with humility and as much openness as possible, to learn to draw the line between incorporating the vision of others and standing firm with the vision we have. I have found it immensely liberating to determine to make the best judgements I can before God, and then to leave the outcome to him. Practically never do I attempt to

persuade someone not to resign if they are threatening to do so; or not to leave if that is how they
are thinking.

'They went out from us, for they were not of us'
is what the apostle John says about heretics. We
have honestly not had any heretics leave us, and
very few wolves in sheep's clothing. The vast
majority of those who have left have been people
who no longer fitted with the personality of the
church. Every church, just like every individual,
develops their own personality. Although maturity
involves a stretching of that personality, character
is by no means lost in healthy development. We
have sought to grow a mature and rounded personality for St Thomas's, but nothing can alter the
fact that some people fit with it and others do not.
A church, just like each one of us, has in the final
issue to be true to itself.

With one or two exceptions, the departure of
members out of disagreement or disharmony with
us has been a mutual sadness, yet also a gain to
both. Both sides tend to find freedom in the wake
of parting company. Indeed I have discovered that
when there is division in the church God takes
sides: he is for both sides!

When I am now asked for my advice about which
church someone should join my reply is as follows.
Unless God has given you clear guidance to the
contrary (and sometimes he does) find out the
direction the leadership is taking. If you can agree
with that direction, then go with them, however
terrible the present state of the church is. If, on the
other hand, you cannot agree with that direction,
then do not join, however wonderful the present
state of the church may be. The reason is that you

will always end up in the ranks of the opposition, and in the life of the church I have never seen either a happy or a successful opposition. Go where you can say 'amen' to the direction of the church.

Those leaving us now (and the growth of the church indicates that they are the exception, rather than the rule) get a better deal than their predecessors did. This is not due to our greater size, but fuller experience. We avoid long theological arguments, strained relationships, or desperate attempts to keep everyone happy. I also seek to avoid taking such departures personally — though it usually still hurts. What we do, whenever possible, is to send people out with our blessing. Recently, on two separate occasions, most members of a fellowship group decided to leave the church. With both groups I made contact with the new minister and asked if this group could become one of their recognised home groups. Both ministers welcomed the approach, and the groups.

Acts 15

Many of the principles I have outlined here can be seen mirrored in the account of the Council of Jerusalem in Acts 15. God was clearly at work, and the church met to talk together across the divide that marked their varied response to what was happening. They met to discover what action to take because they were a church seeking to keep moving in God's purposes.

The discernment came through a two-fold practice of listening. They listened to stories and testimonies of God's grace at work in the lives of Gentiles; and they listened to the scriptures as they saw them being fulfilled before their eyes.

The amount of discussion and the sense of to and fro in debate in these verses is evidence of the way they were seeking to face, and come to terms with, their feelings about the unprecedented happenings among them, not least of which was the radical change in theology that God, through events, seemed to be forcing upon them. 'Then Gentiles also are heirs of grace.' What a cultural bombshell, and vast emotional shock. Nonetheless, they held firm to what they discerned as God's plan, not to what they thought was possible. Politics is the art of the possible; Christianity, they were demonstrating, is the art of the impossible.

Their decision gave as much freedom as possible: 'It has seemed good to the Holy Spirit and to us to lay upon you no other burden than these necessary things ...' Their attention was on how simple they could keep any necessary rules, and how free they could let others be. They gave them headroom and space to express their faith in a way appropriate to them.

The debate was set in the context of a spiritual battle which Paul expounds in his letter to the Galatians. Sharp words were no doubt spoken, and in the end the leaders sought not so much to find how to keep everyone happy, as how to obey God. It created its own division, no doubt, with some of the circumcision party continuing to oppose the decision, and maybe setting up on their own. The leaders were not afraid to grasp the nettle and exercise leadership: they would have had to face the prospect of letting go of some of their members. Though a few were troubled, the whole body was healed. Such is the way that the people of God hold together.

Acts 15 has a sober ending. It is a chapter that is always associated with that tremendous manifestation of unity between Jewish and Gentile believers in the Jerusalem Council. However the final verses record the sad story of the way that Paul and Barnabas fell out over Mark. Yet, even there, redemption breaks through. Mark got just what he needed: discipline *and* the chance to prove himself. The number of mission teams doubled, and in the long run Paul and Barnabas and Mark were reconciled and the purposes of God achieved. Grace meets us in just the same way today even in our broken relationships; thanks be to God!

Chapter Ten

SHAKING

The story of the church's development in the first half of the 1980s is not an easy one to tell — for two reasons. First, it was quite complex, with a series of different elements and cross-currents in it. The tide was not all going the same way. Second, it contained some painful and disturbing times that it would be easier not to write about. However, they are part of the story, and need both to be owned and told. Not least is that so because much of the growth that happened after this period was built on the solid foundations that were forged through a period of testing and shaking.

The period began quietly enough, after the celebrations associated with the re-opening of the new St Thomas's, on Saturday December 13, 1980.

Moving back from the Baptist church and settling in took time. We now had to adjust to having a parish office, and a new church administrator — Jean Stranex, who had joined us from Tear Fund. It was a big change for me to have an office at church and no longer to be working from home. I had reserved the right to move back home if it did not work out, but that was not necessary. It worked well; as did the whole church's adjustment to the new building. Initially during worship, however, I found myself lost in all the space after two years of coping with the very cramped conditions of the Baptist church.

Life left us little enough time to readjust and settle in.

In the leadership it was all change. Eric France, Richard Laughlin and I were all very tired and in need of rest. I was due to have a sabbatical starting at Easter 1981. Eric and Richard were both overdue to stand down as churchwardens, having stayed on to see the building project through to completion. Because Richard had also been the treasurer we were to change that vital position too. In addition, David Hughes, who was to lead the staff team during my time away, was himself preparing for a move.

As if all that upheaval was not enough, this virtually new team of David Hughes as acting vicar, with two new churchwardens and a new treasurer, were required to tackle some major tasks. One was to purchase a new house, and arrange for it to be put in good decorative state and working order for John Marsh, who was to replace David Hughes. Then, in the spring of that year, the imminent prospect of a new building project, with the purchase and re-ordering of the next-door Crookes Endowed School, suddenly burst upon the scene. This was not what we had been seeking!

Crookes Endowed Centre

The cost of purchasing the building was thirty thousand pounds. We expected to have to pay as much again to renovate it. In the final issue it would cost nearly one hundred thousand pounds to complete the work. We decided that God was not calling the church to another major financial sacrifice, but rather that we should seek to find the money for this work through trust funds and the variety of government agencies at the time. We saw the involvement of the church as coming later, through the giving of ourselves in service to others, once the building was available.

Paul Wells, who had joined the staff in 1978 as a lay evangelist, had proved his considerable gifts and ability in approaching trust funds during the church extension project. He now took on a futher round of approaches to such groups. The fact that what we were doing was classed as a community centre, rather than church, made it much more attractive to most trust funds.

Costs continually escalated way beyond original estimates. Our prayers for funding from sources outside the church were not fully answered. We had the problem of having a building before we had a fully developed plan of how to use it. At one point it became a separate power centre and was in danger of operating over against the church. We continue to struggle with how best to balance lettings that pay an economic rent, with the desire and call to serve the community, the need to find additional space for the rapid growth of many church activities, and the pressing need for more office space. It is a tension we are, however, seeing the need to live with rather than solve in some over-simple way.

Growth

As soon as we moved back into the new church building at the end of 1980 we began to see growth. By the time we had moved back our usual Sunday attendance had risen to over four hundred and seventy people. We had added one hundred of those during the five years of the building project. By the end of 1983, just three years after returning, we had added the best part of another two hundred, and were by then seeing six hundred and fifty people in church every Sunday. Those figures are the average for the whole year, including holiday times and times when we have virtually no students. For much of the year we were having seven or eight hundred a Sunday.

That growth was to create problems. We had not really come to terms with the implications of being a large church, and now, of course, it was a lot less risky to be part of the church than during the extension project. We were soon to enter another crucible experience and Gideon-like shake out.

Danger Signs

A few astute people, including Ann, had seen signs of problems well before most of us did.

One of the first was to do with the very success of the building project. A very clear (indeed, concrete) goal had been set before us. There was an all too obvious job for each of us to do — to pray and to give. It united us all. But what was now to unite us? We had said that the kingdom of God is more important than buildings, but when it came to the crunch we had great problems defining what we meant by the kingdom. It seemed just the opposite of the building project. We had changed from concrete to mist as the medium we were working in.

Furthermore, the focus of attention of the church before the building project was on our own experience of God. Good and necessary though that was, it was inward looking. As we turned outwards, to be extended into the community, we hardly knew what to do, where to go, or how to proceed.

A marvellous quotation, that I came across subsequently, sums up our instinctive reaction as a staff team to this situation. It reads as follows:

> We trained hard but it seems that every time we
> were beginning to form into teams we would be
> re-organised. I was to learn, later in life,
> that we tend to meet any new situation by
> re-organising, and a wonderful method it can be
> for creating the illusion of progress while
> producing confusion, inefficiency and demoralisation.

It sounds so uncannily modern, yet it was actually written by Petronius Arbiter, a Roman, in AD66. It described just what we did.

We produced a document spelling out all the changes we were to make in order to release more people for service in the community. The idea was fine enough, but in reality it was simply reorganisation. We had to learn that, vital though structures are to *contain* a work of God, they are no good at *creating* one. All we really achieved was a fairly destructive effect on the fellowship groups. This happened because of the decision to downgrade the role of leader to convenor. It actually played little part in releasing people into service; it just made our fellowship groups struggle. It has taken four years to recover the situation.

The truth was that we had, to a very considerable degree, run out of spiritual life and energy. It was not surprising in view of all the demands that had been upon us during the building project. With hindsight I now see that we would have been better advised to have taken time to come back to God, be renewed and refreshed in our faith, and then moved on.

Finally, we got ourselves into a situation where we were working on a double or triple agenda. Our Finishing The Task gift day for the building project was scheduled for June. In January we added the few thousand pounds shortfall on the Crookes Endowed Centre to the target for that day. We then launched into a major visitation of the whole parish in the two months around that gift day. By the time the gift day was upon us the Crookes Endowed Centre bill had risen to £25,000. We were now needing a total of £50,000 on the day. The giving of £27,000 was a wonderful expression of giving, yet it was nowhere near our target. Cross-currents of thanksgiving and disappointment swirled around the church. Like a cat extricating itself from the mess it has made with a ball of wool, the tangle was increasing with every move.

Areas

A complicating factor in the situation was the development of 'areas'. We had established these while we were worshipping in the Baptist church. They were a response to the growth of the church, and the multiplication of the number of supporting fellowships. In order to handle this growth we divided the parish into three (originally four) areas, and grouped the fellowship groups in that part of the parish together. It provided an intermediate grouping between the small fellowship and the large Sunday services. Each area had one or two staff members involved in its leadership.

In order to make way for mid-week area meetings we had discontinued the mid-week fellowship. For some people the areas were a great joy, and just the size of grouping that they could most easily relate to. They served a valuable purpose in helping us to get to know newcomers more quickly.

Shaking

At the very beginning of this period (March 1981) the groups from one of the areas went away for a weekend at which Tom Smail came and spoke about the fatherhood of God. In the closing communion service, after a happy and refreshing weekend, Tom Smail spoke a disturbing prophecy which surprised us all. It did not seem to relate to anything he had taught about, not did it seem to connect with the state of the church at that time. It was a clear and brief word which went as follows:

There is a great shaking ahead for you.

Because God has built well a great shaking will come to the church.

Everything not attached to the foundation will come tumbling down. Everything attached to the foundation will stand.

Every church has its problems, and on a number of occasions in the coming year we said to ourselves, 'This is the shaking;' but it was not. That did not come until over two years later. We had not been used to such a long time-fuse on a prophecy before. By the time it began to be fulfilled we had set it on one side as something we must have passed without noticing. When it came there was no way anyone could miss it.

'Troubles never come alone', and that was to be our experience. We had what I can only describe as a multiple pile-up. It is out of this experience that I often point out to those looking longingly at a church like St Thomas's that 'the only difference between a small church and a large church is in the number and size of the problems.'

First, we hit financial problems. Because our growth had been steady and undramatic, we had not properly adjusted to the fact that we were now a large organisation and needed to change the way we handled our money. We had not established any rules about who could authorise expenditure for what. Too many people were doing so, and too many decisions were being made without any awareness of the financial implications. We had not developed very effective accounting methods either, so we were £20,000 into the red before we were alerted. We learnt the hard way that large churches need to change style and structure to adapt to new demands. Having been blessed so much in the financial area as a church we were not well equipped to tackle such a problem.

When, in December 1983, we first clearly grasped the extent of the financial problem we went back to the church. We were hoping for a major

increase in giving. None was forthcoming. A sense
of dissatisfaction about the state of the church had
led to the supply of money levelling off. Rather
than rebuke the church for failing to meet the
challenge, we took it as God's word to the
leadership that greater income was not the way that
the problem was to be solved. We needed to face
the other problems, rather than spend our way out
of difficulties.

Second, we ran into area problems. The grouping
of fellowship groups into areas had initially looked
very promising, but we began to hit problems.
Having abandoned the mid-week fellowship to
make room for area meetings we had nowhere we
could listen to God, hear his word to us, or honestly
face up to problems, as a whole church.

We were also finding that areas and fellowship
groups were in tension about how to use our
mid-week time together. We tried monthly area
meetings, followed by three weeks for fellowship
groups, but area leaders did not feel that was
enough. We tried alternating area and fellowship
meetings, but fellowship groups complained about
the lack of continuity in their meetings. We even
went to a complex six-week rota with two fellowship weeks, followed by an area meeting, etc. It
was a good idea — except that no one could
remember which week we were in, or where we
were meant to be. As a result of this some were
saying that the problem with areas was that we had
not given them enough space and we ought to be
bold and form three separate churches. A small
group in one area became enthusiastic for that. The
majority were feeling the opposite. Their conclusion was that areas had not worked. We were in

disarray.

Third, we were faced with the problems of growth.
Although we had broken through the one-man
ministry barrier that often blocks the growth of a
church beyond the number that one man can relate
to (under two hundred people), we had not made
any great adjustments since that time. Yet we were
now three times that size. Our existing ways of
operating were stretched to the limits, as were the
relationships on which those structures depended.

Fourth, we were handling the problems of success.
Right then it felt like anything but successful.
However the reality was just that. This needs some
explanation. It has to do with living by faith and
living by sight.

When a church is struggling, when the building is
crumbling and the congregation grumbling, when
both the plaster and the attendances are falling,
everyone knows, can see and feel, that there are
problems. Sight is an aid to faith (as long as it does
not lead to despair). In those circumstances everything is shouting aloud to us that we need God's
help — and fast. However, when the heating
works, the congregations are growing, the building
is bright, warm and attractive, and the place
humming with activity, our environment can become an enemy to faith. Those positive circumstances can begin to signal all sorts of false messages,
such as: 'Haven't we done well!', 'We are doing
rather nicely', and even 'You can leave this one to
us now, God'. This profound shift in what our
circumstances are saying is the inevitable result of
growth in a work of God. It is the fundamental
problem the children of Israel faced as they entered
the Promised Land. God sought to prepare them,

and alert them to the dangers ahead.

> When you eat and are satisfied, when you build fine houses and settle down, and when your herds and flocks grow large ... do not forget the Lord your God who brought you out of Egypt, out of the land of slavery ... Otherwise you may say to yourself, 'My power and the strength of my hands have produced this wealth for me.' But remember the Lord your God, for it is he who gives you the ability to produce wealth, and so confirms his covenant.
> (Exodus 8.12-18)

Their growth was a good thing, the gift of God. The danger lay in allowing their circumstances to tell them the opposite. This arrival syndrome was part of the problem we were encountering.

Fifth, we were encountering spiritual problems. With hindsight I see that the renewal of the 1970s was running out of steam, but this was masked by all that was going on: the building project, the Crookes Endowed Centre, the local ecumenical project. We had lost a sense of direction, our first love for the Lord, and spiritual momentum. We were, in terms of catching the wind of the Spirit, in the doldrums (dictionary definition: 'where calms and baffling winds prevail: low spirits').

Sixth, and most importantly, we hit leadership problems. The staff team got into a tangle over something we called corporate leadership but was definitely something else. I now see it as defective in theory as it proved to be unworkable in practice. It was a form of group democracy in which the decision went to him who pushed hardest. I felt my personality rubbed out in the process, so when the pile-up occurred I was in no state to deal with the

situation clearly, decisively or effectively. The ship
was now drifting close to the rocks, and the captain
was incapacitated.

The Crunch

The whole situation came to a head in January
1984. We had already pruned our expenditure to an
absolute minimum but the differences were margin-
al. Without a reduction in staff size we would not be
able either to cover our losses or balance our books
for the coming year. The church council had twice
met to discuss the proposal that, in view of our
financial situation, we had to reduce the staff team
by two. We had failed to grasp the nettle and were
now meeting again. Some were eager for swift and
decisive action, others wanted us to wait; a good
number were confused and indecisive. In the
meanwhile, at short notice and in response to a
prophecy, the church had been called to a week of
prayer. Typical of the confusion of the situation,
that week began on the same Monday evening as
the council meeting. Some on the council argued
that we should be in the prayer meeting and that
the council meeting should be postponed again.

The decision was taken that night to reduce the
staff team by two.

A couple of weeks later a series of events on a
single day enabled me to break out of the passive
mode in which I had become trapped. Terry Pratt
attended a staff meeting and helped me to see what
was going on. Someone rang me to share a scripture
that put the whole situation into sharp focus. Chris
Brain, the leader of a rock group associated with
the church, rang to remind me of what I had said to

him a year previously when he was going through struggles in the leadership of that group. Finally, at a meal with friends, I was able to express what I was feeling, and was able to step out of the shell of unreality.

It was a difficult experience for many, and I personally found it very painful. I knew I was close to breaking point and found great release in tears. By the grace of God, and a series of radical decisions, we pulled through. But not before two staff members were asked to find other employment, the house of one of them (which the church owned) was sold to pay off our debts, and the areas experiment was abandoned with a real sense of regret (as well as relief). To our surprise, and relief, the church held together rather than fell apart under the impact of these events. About six people left the church as a result of what had happened: though some of us bear the scars to this day.

Recognising that each one of us, as part of the one community of believers, had contributed in some way to the problems we were in, we held a special act of repentance set in a communion service on Ash Wednesday 1984. When it came to the confession we were all invited to write down, on paper provided, what we felt our own part in the troubles we were going through had been. We then proceeded out of the back of the worship area, through the lounge to the patio area outside. There a dustbin had been placed and newspaper put in the bottom and set on fire. Each of us, beginning with me, dropped our 'sins' in the bin, as a physical sign to us both of our repentance and God's forgiveness.

Personal Growth

'Churches die from the top down; they die when their leaders die.' Those were the words of George Carey, Bishop of Bath and Wells, at a day conference on church planting within the Church of England, which I attended. It echoed my own uncomfortable experience that a church can grow only as much as its leader (and leadership) grows. This meant that the first place to look for a move forward would be in me as a person.

I had found the whole experience a shattering one, but also one through which I learnt lessons, and have changed as a person. I now confront problems earlier, and do not believe that patience and understanding are all that is needed to deal with every problem. Sometimes tough decisions, not least about people, are what leadership demands. I also learnt the difference between the abdication and delegation of responsibility; and that authority can only be shared when you are clear that it is yours to share. I was made uncomfortably aware of the fact that growing as a person is the necessary precondition for the growth of the church.

I thought about why God was touching me at the point of my weaknesses, and realised that he loves me more than I do. I am content with my failings, and blind spots, and prejudices. I have learnt to accept them and live with them. However, God loves me more than I do and is committed to helping me move out of these things.

This pattern of God's handling his people is evident from the scriptures. He is so committed to the holiness and wholeness, the growth and fruitfulness, of his servants, that he is willing to take them through painful experiences to achieve those goals. Abraham must wait nearly quarter of a century for the child of promise, and then be willing to sacrifice the gift he has been given by God, in order for him to become the father of faith. Moses must experience rejection for his headstrong solutions to the needs of God's people, and then wait for forty years, before he can become the man God can use to set God's people free. David, though called and anointed king, must run and hide for his life from Saul for many years before God can make of him the man he wanted to be the king of Israel. In all these people and in us, God is more committed to the goal of growth than to our comfort and ease along the way, because of his love. They all found how uncomfortable it is to be loved by someone who loved them more than they did themselves.

The same pattern is at work in those who preach the message of the incarnation. That message of God's power to redeem human nature needs to be demonstrated in us, especially in those of us called into leadership.

Over the years I have discovered that I can never have a true understanding of what God is wanting to do in my ministry, unless I broaden my vision enough to ask what is he wanting to do in me: how am I to grow? So, without indulging in introspection, a time of plateau in the life of the church indicates now that I need to be listening afresh to the Lord, to discover the growth points he is wanting to work on in me. We like to focus on our strengths and minister out of them. For our wholeness, God seems more often to have his attention on our weaknesses, so that they can be faced, redeemed, and turned into new strengths by his grace and to his glory.

Turning Round

We took two years to come through the experience, and we found it important to let people go over what had happened for sometime afterwards in order for us to work through some of the painful feelings and broken relationships that had resulted. We had to take time and care to put personal relationships right, because harsh and judgemental things had been said and done, and we needed to seek forgiveness from each other.

We re-established the leadership of the church with a clear recognition that every team needs a leader with freedom and authority to lead. We also saw that the staff team, who exercise much of the leadership within the church, need themselves to be both properly pastored, and also fully accountable to others for their work — both as a team, and individually. The three wardens (including the Baptist warden) have now been given this responsibility, which is being developed all the time.

Corporate prayer was restored to its central place in the life of the church by the introduction of a central prayer meeting. It has been a vital means of communication of both problems and vision with the whole church. We have put considerable thought and prayer into how best to run such a meeting, which by 1988 was regularly drawing over three hundred people. How to handle a prayer meeting of that size is not easy to discover, but the very numbers attending underline the importance the whole church now attaches to praying together.

The difficult decision to discontinue the areas was hard, because they had been of value in enabling people not to be lost in a large church. Many strong relationships had been built in these groups. However, they had only been able to get us so far, and we decided that the problems were terminal. What was particularly difficult was taking the step of faith of leaving a pastoral vacuum by not proposing an instant substitute. I, for one, was sure that the areas had been meeting a real need. However, I was sure from previous experience that the only right course was to stop the areas, wait on God, and see what shape vacuum was created by their absence.

Our financial management was radically altered, as a result of John Goepel (one of the churchwardens) stepping in to deal with the problems we faced. We established budgets for each section of the church's life, and clearly recognised budget holders. They were to be responsible for presenting budgets in the autumn for the coming year; for authorising expenditure through the year, and for ensuring that the amount allocated was not exceeded. We have put a very considerable amount of time into computerising all our accounts so that we have an early warning system of any impending problem.

We had also to learn that there is no such thing as having 'arrived' in the Christian faith. We could not rely on the fact that in the past we had been a generous, or loving church. Our only hope was in trusting God to keep us in those good things that had happened among us, and to restore them to us when we lost them. Reputation was as lethal to us as it was to the church of Laodicea.

Over the three years from the end of 1983 to the end of 1986 we saw no growth in the usual Sunday attendance. In fact it dropped by ten in 1984, and regained that number in 1985. We had seen before that, when growth levels off, God is drawing attention to some underlying problem which needs to be dealt with before growth can move on. On this occasion we were well aware of what the problems were.

It is testimony both to the grace of God, and to the patience and maturity of the church, that I can write in this way about a time of failure. We were learning again what we had learnt during the building project, that our problems were not a frustrating obstacle to our getting on with the real work of proclaiming the gospel. Rather they were the means God was using to apply the gospel to real life situations.

This part of the story is recorded not least as testimony to the fact that God is able to take his church through difficult and testing times, maturing and purifying it in the process. Our experience has been that, because God, not man, is the head of the church, he can be trusted enough for us to face failure and sin, look it in the face, own our part in it, and see his redeeming work.

The gospel is good news, to the individual and to communities, that sin and failure, if faced and owned, can be redeemed.

Chapter Eleven

GROWING

In January 1985 the staff team took to the church council the idea of dividing the morning service into two in order to create more space for newcomers. The idea was resisted, and finally rejected on the grounds that we were having enough problems manning one service and would not be able to find the manpower for two. I did not agree with that, but it was evident that it was not the right time to seek to move on this. I was happy to wait for a better moment, though I could not see what might bring it about.

One of the reasons for it not being the right moment was that it was going in the opposite direction from where people were emotionally. Our troubles of the previous few years had been a painful time, and there was need for us to come together, rather than move into some form of division.

We needed also to face honestly the question of whether we should be holding together as one church, or dividing into several smaller ones. Certainly there were some valid reasons for dividing. Growth had seemed to result in a more organisational, even bureaucratic, form of church life. It seemed inevitable. For example, in a small church the leader of the children's work can know everyone well enough to know who to avoid and who to go after to seek their help in the work. With over six hundred worshippers by this time there was no way that that was possible. So we had to send letters to fellowship group leaders to ask them to suggest names and share the need. It felt impersonal. The sense of being a church family seemed to be fading.

While the staff were talking about creating space for newcomers, and enabling the growth of the church to take off again, the mood in the church was 'Help, stop, we are too big already!' It was understandable enough.

One Church

The first task, therefore, was to address the central question as to whether God was calling us to hold together as one church, or whether we should be looking for ways of dividing into smaller ones. It was not something that we talked about at any length with the whole church, or even the church council, but I knew that I had to be clear in my own mind about this before we could move forward.

We came back again to consider 'what the Father is doing', and to see the direction in which he was leading. It quickly emerged that the signposts were all pointing in the same direction.

The geographical size of the parish is small. Daughter churches, whether of the traditional sort or of an informal church-planting type, were ruled out by the compactness of the parish. From hardly anywhere in it does it take more than ten minutes to walk to church.

Our buildings pointed in the same direction too. It really made no sense for the Baptists to have demolished their building if we were now going to be planting smaller churches in the area. Moreover, the whole work of the church extension project, and the establishing of the Crookes Endowed Centre, had given us very considerable church plant: ideal for a large church, but hopeless for smaller ones. God had manifestly led us in these projects and yet if we were to divide they would be a millstone around one of the church's necks. Moreover, the development of youth work, with a full-time worker, which these buildings enabled us to do, was only possible from the base of a large church. That too would be in jeopardy if we split into several smaller groups.

Over the years we have been able to give support, practical help and inspiration to many of the smaller churches around us. We have seen this as an important part of our calling. We had also been able to give these churches new members. Our transfer ratio (the number of those leaving us to join other churches compared with the number of people leaving other churches to join us) had consistently been five to one. We were in the export business!

Finally, we realised that neither the leadership, nor the vast majority of the church, had any desire or sense of call from God to divide. Those dozen or so members who were expressing such things were doing so in order to express dissatisfaction with the state of the church. We needed to listen to that, rather than act on the solution they were proposing.

So our commitment to hold together was established. Now, we could give our attention to solving the problems we faced in being a large church. However, we had not got far in the process before a major breath of new life was to sweep through us, and change our perspectives, and the shape and size of the problems.

Wimber

As we came out of these troubles two major events were due to take place in Sheffield in 1985. First was Billy Graham's Mission Sheffield, the second was John Wimber's signs and wonders conference. I had been significantly affected by the ministry of both men.

I was very much in favour of Billy Graham coming (not least because of the impact of his ministry on our family back in the 1950s) and encouraged Paul Wells in the part he played to bring this about. In the providence of God not only did Billy Graham come, but the full-time work of organisation fitted Paul's gifts and his need for a job when we decided to reduce the staff team.

I knew the weaknesses of crusade evangelism. Our own growth had come about through an every-member approach. I was involved with my heart rather than my mind. As a church we were fully involved. A gift day produced £12,000 for the mission; we took several double-decker buses every night; many of our people organised the steward-ing, helped with the choir, and were specialist counsellors. It was good to be involved, not least as a service to others, but the fruit was meagre. About twenty people came to faith, which was less than our yearly average, and certainly less than if we had put all that energy and manpower into personal evangelism. Our statistics showed no discernible growth that year; though coming through the time of shaking was the primary influence on that fact.

I encountered John Wimber for the first time in the autumn of 1985 at his signs and wonders conference in the Central Hall, Westminster. I found John's teaching compelling. It had a clear philosophical base which connected with so much of my earlier involvement with Francis Schaeffer. I warmed to his open, honest questioning yet faith-filled approach to scripture as the test of every-thing. I found his own handling of super-star pressure delightful: he didn't need to be successful.

In the course of the conference, in fact in my room in London after one of the workshops, God met with me. I experienced a cleansing, forgive-ness, and renewed commissioning before the Lord. I found myself deeply refreshed and ready again both for ministry in the power of the Spirit at a new level, and for the whole challenge of the ministry.

That was in the autumn of 1984. A couple of weeks afterwards, sensing that the key to all John Wimber had taught lay in prayer, I rang Bishop David Pytches of St Andrew's, Chorleywood, to see if I could get hold of some 'Wimber tapes' on prayer. I did not get them: but I did get much more. David asked me simply, 'If John Wimber was to come back again, where should he come?' 'Shef-field!' I said, before stopping to think of the implications. And so with one word I found myself involved in organising a number of such confer-ences in the North of England.

The first one was in Sheffield City Hall in October 1985. By the time it took place, the three of us from the staff team who had been to Westminster (myself, David Dewey and John Marsh) had sought to share all we knew, which was little enough. First, in the January of that year, we called forty or so leaders of the church together and taught and practised what we had learnt about how to pray while watching to 'see what the Father is doing'. It included time to invite the Spirit to come and work among us. We met with a largely positive, believing and supportive response from those leaders.

That was followed by a series of 'Kingdom Workshops' in the May and September of that year when, at 8.30pm on a Sunday evening, we followed the three-fold pattern of worship-word-ministry with the several hundred members of the church who came. God moved in power on each occasion and many experienced God in a new way.

Two particular incidents stick in my mind. The first time we invited the Holy Spirit to come someone almost immediately had a word of knowledge about someone with some specific back problem. We had said we would wait until we had several such words before praying for anyone. However, one women put her hand up immediately. She did this several times, and so I thought I should call her forward since she seemed so keen. Later I learnt that the movement of her hand was entirely involuntary. She kept putting it down, but it kept going back up again!

As soon as we began to pray for her she fell to the ground. We continued to pray for her and within minutes she was up on her feet with no symptoms of the trouble. What delighted me most was that the next day she was heard shouting over the fence to a friend: 'He came to me while I was on the floor in church last night.' Here attention was not on the experience, or even on the healing, but on the God who had come to her.

The other incident involved a woman who came very wary of what was going on and determined to keep out of trouble. She sat at the back of the church with her coat on ready to make a quick exit. She may not have felt ready for the Holy Spirit to meet her in a dramatic way, but he was ready for her. The Spirit came upon her so powerfully that she fell to the floor — right across the doorway. Everyone saw her as they had to step over her on the way out. How different is God's way of working from our plans!

In due course we became relaxed about such dramatic outward signs as people falling to the ground (sometimes called 'resting', or being 'slain' in the Spirit). The first time it happened someone called for a doctor because they thought the person must have fainted. We quickly learnt that outward dramatic events were no guide to the significance of what was taking place in a person's life. Sometimes it was a sign of great things to come, and at other times it was the only occurrence. As often as not God worked in power without any outward signs. We certainly discouraged seeking an experience for its own sake. 'Seek the Lord and you will receive all you need and all you can handle', was our approach.

With these events behind us the church was quite well prepared to take advantage of the signs and wonders conference in the city hall. There were over two thousand people there, of whom nearly one hundred were from St Thomas's.

It was this, and the team visit by one of the Vineyard teams in the three days following, that was to launch us into the strongest thrust of growth that any of us had yet seen.

Signs and Wonders

The central thrust of John Wimber's teaching is focused on restoring the supernatural dimension to Christianity. Four particular marks of his teaching stand out.

First, is the fact that western Christianity has allowed the gospel to be squeezed into a rationalistic and mechanical world-view. This is something that writers like Harry Blamires, Francis Schaeffer and Lesslie Newbigin, have been drawing the church's attention to for some while.

Second, the kingdom is the central theme of Jesus's teaching and understanding of the healing ministry. Jesus thought in terms of the age to come invading this age with the wholeness of heaven. In the process he was doing battle with the evil forces at work in what the Prayer Book calls 'this naughty world'.

Third, Jesus proclaimed the coming of the kingdom by both words and works. He healed, cast out demons, raised the dead, and did nature miracles as part of his proclamation of the kingdom.

Fourth, Jesus trained his disciples to continue this kingdom ministry with words and works. The gospels give considerable emphasis to this training process. First they watched Jesus doing it; then they did it with him watching, and finally they were sent out to do it without him. We are called into the same work.

Within the two years after the 1985 conference, particularly through a series of teaching and training weekends mounted by our curate, John Leach, several hundred people had been training in this pattern of healing ministry. They included a large number of people from other churches.

In St Thomas's we gave time for such prayer at the end of most services, and established teams of people to exercise this ministry. Many have encountered God through such times; though we are most encouraged when we hear of such ministry being exercised in fellowship groups, and out in secular environments.

Northern Lights

We found ourselves as a church thrust into a leadership role not only in the John Wimber conferences, but also in handling follow-up days. We quickly established a pattern of such days and found the interest so great that we had to repeat each one (usually on the Wednesday and Thursday of the same week) and ask people not to come twice. In this way we regularly minister to seven or eight hundred people a time. Our focus was particularly on helping churches in the north of England to establish this ministry.

I also set up a leaders' day as a one-off event. We offered a buffet lunch, expecting twenty or thirty people. One hundred and fifty leaders and spouses turned up, which stretched more than our catering arrangements. Since then those days have been continued on a termly basis and are aimed at strengthening the hand of ministers seeking to move in the supernatural realm.

Other days were to follow, as well as invitations to take teams to other churches. John Leach was to take out a number of such teams to good effect. It was all part of what we sensed that God was calling us to do: to give away all that we had learnt and received; again, with particular focus on the north of England, to become a resource centre for others.

Congregations

Within six months of the Wimber conference in Sheffield growth was again taking place after the plateau in 1984 and 1985. We knew that one of the obstacles to growth was when a feeling of 'church full' became evident. Usually this takes place at about eighty-five per cent capacity of the building. That had been an important part of the inspiration and motivation for the building project. However, we were not eager to solve the problem with another such project!

We needed to find a way in which growth could take place without the whole church feeling daunted, and people becoming lost in the crowd. This meant finding how to function in smaller groups rather than a whole church, without adding another tier of church activities or dividing into separate churches.

Sometimes, in smaller churches, the members and leaders look at larger churches and wish they were like them. We were looking at smaller churches and wishing we were like them!

They have such strengths. When, for example, a small church is about to have a harvest festival, everyone is involved and that is important in

building up relationships and a sense of belonging
and unity. We were finding that the opposite was
happening. First, the place appeared to be running
smoothly, and many people felt 'they don't need
me'. In any case, with hundreds of people around,
there will always be someone who is keener to do it
than I am, and is better at it. Second, when
someone did get involved, it did not, in our
situation, build relationships. They might not meet
that group of people for months on end. This meant
that, thirdly, the focus was on getting the job done,
rather than on growing together. As a result, an
activity such as a harvest festival became counter-
productive: a chore that reinforced our lack of
relationships with most other members of the
church.

Into this situation came the idea of turning each
Sunday service into a pastoral unit; a congregation.
They would become our new 'areas'. One of the
exciting things about this was that we achieved what
we wanted to with areas without adding a single
additional meeting.

As the plans developed we included the principle
of looking to divide both the morning service
(10.30am), which was already full with virtually no
room for growth, and in due course the evening
service (6.30pm).

Making congregations pastoral units involved
two important steps.

*First, we saw the need for each congregation to
have its own network of fellowship groups.* However, we decided not to have a 'big bang' approach
and change all groups at one go, but simply to allow
a process of natural development in this direction.
It is still too early to know whether this will be

sufficient.

Second, we would need to encourage everyone to be committed to one congregation. This would be their choice, and might well change, but we needed to know who was pastorally responsible for them. It would not, of course, mean that they could not attend other services. In fact some are involved in one service and then stay on, or help in the children's work, in another. Others do it the other way round, helping in some ministry in their congregation and joining in the worship at another time.

Leadership

We saw the need for a team of leaders for each congregation. With the plan to divide the morning service into two (from 10.30am to 9.15am and 11.15am) in September 1987, we would need three teams, and three team leaders. It took us surprisingly long to see the, now obvious, answer to who should be congregational leaders. With an additional curate allowed at Easter 1987, the new Baptist minister, and Steve Lee, the youth leader (who had himself established two congregations while on mission service in Lima), we had three congregational leaders.

Each leadership team has a staff member as congregational leader, and then a group of lay leaders fulfilling various roles. The congregational pastor, with a team of two or three pastoral leaders, has responsibility for the care of all those in the congregation and especially for oversight of the supporting fellowships. The ministry leader helps in the process of recruiting and strengthening the church's service of the community, working with the other congregational ministry leaders to develop the overall shape of the church's service. The welcome pastors are responsible for welcoming newcomers and integrating them into the church. The congregational organisers are there to ensure that services, and congregational events, are run efficiently.

Those teams were given responsibility for the pastoral, social, and evangelistic side of the congregation's life. The overall direction of the whole church, together with the teaching ministry and leading of worship, was to remain the responsibility of the whole staff team, thus helping in the process of holding together.

We set this leadership structure in what is technically called a *matrix leadership pattern*. This means that responsibilities go in two directions. The ministry leader, for example, not only works within the congregational leadership team under the direction of the congregational leader; but he or she also works in the whole church team of ministry leaders on whole-church issues. For the staff members who are congregational leaders this means that they also have some whole-church responsibility, such as our mid-week training programme or weddings, the youth work or the development of the church's ministry in the community. It is like the warp and weft of a piece of material. In the discussion paper in which I first set this out I ended with the question: 'Will this make for twice the strength, or double the hassle?' Our early experience would suggest that it will do both. Certainly the move into congregations has encouraged initiative and drawn many people into ministry at a deeper level. The hassle is part of the price of seeking to hold together as one church.

Holding Together

We were stepping out in an unusual direction, and doing what most churches fight hard to resist; allowing each congregation to become a separate and distinct grouping. In doing this it was going to be important to build into the way we functioned both freedom for congregations to develop their own life, and yet also a clear sense of being one church and working together as one. We identified several ways in which unity would be sustained.

The primary integrating factor is our commitment to work together on the one vision that God is giving to us as a whole church. We seek to discover and discern this in a multitude of ways. However, having one staff team and a monthly central prayer meeting are vital elements in this.

Another way of holding together is through the matrix leadership pattern I have described above.

A further way of holding the whole church together is through the development of whole-church ministry teams. These are groups of people working on some aspect of the church's ministry (such as youth work, or care of the elderly), in which the members of that ministry team are from all the different congregations.

We plan to hold whole church celebrations, though so far have had problems finding a suitable, and available, place in which they could be held. The idea would be to hold three such events a year. They would take place on Sunday. None of the congregations would hold their own services. We would all combine together in one major event.

We moved into congregations in September 1987. It was a major operation. Each congregation needed not only to develop its own leadership team, but also to discover people willing to serve in a number of ways. We now would have three worship teams, three stewarding teams, and three teams of people to man the amplification equipment and overhead projector. We also had to establish a new set of children's work teams totalling fifty people in all. It was a major and time-consuming undertaking which took the whole summer to achieve. But, when the time arrived, we were ready enough to start, though manning all the teams of stewards and children's work is a continuing struggle.

For the two morning congregations there was immediate change. A new time, and a smaller group of people to get to know. For the 6.30pm congregation little was to change initially; we were waiting for the arrival in January 1988 of Paddy Mallon, the new Baptist minister.

Right from the start we made it clear that it could take eighteen months for us to settle down fully, and be sure that this was the right way. However, joys, successes and advantages have already greatly outweighed any problems. Within six months each of the congregations was growing quite strongly and the usual Sunday attendance since the congregations were begun has been over one thousand, and growing.

We rejoice in finding the Lord's way through the constraints to growth, and are confident that when the next obstacle comes, he will show us the way through that so that the church may continue to win many more to a living faith in Christ, and equip them to become effective disciples of his in the world today.

Chapter Twelve

NINE O'CLOCK IN THE EVENING

It was a sunny summer afternoon and I was on my way to church to take the lunch-time communion service. This was one of those rare occasions when, apart from funerals and special events, I could be seen wearing a dog collar. As I crossed the main road I was aware of a large Volvo parked beside the road with a disabled person's sticker in the rear window. Coming up to the car, parked with the passenger door by the kerbside, I noticed a wheel-chair in the passenger's seat. As I drew level with the car I heard a voice from inside pleading, 'Give us a hand, guv!'

My readiness to do my boy scout bit was reinforced by the combination of his wheel-chair and my dog collar. The latter left me no option. I assumed the driver wanted me to help him out. However, he leant across the passenger seat, and put his hand out to me through the open window. I was handed two green pieces of paper, one of which was a pound note, and the other looked rather like a receipt of some sort. The man simply said: 'Put this on for me, please guv.'

It was only then that the full horror of the situation dawned upon me. Behind me was the local betting shop. He was wanting me to place a bet for him!

Now was too late to withdraw my offer of help. There was no way that a sermon on the evils of betting was going to work in these circumstances. With a quick look to left, and to right (to check that there were no parishioners, or *That's Life* camera crews in sight) I crossed the pavement swiftly and had my hand on the door in a moment, and just had time to reassure myself that at lunchtime there would quite likely be nobody in.

It was crowded!

What was worse was that it was a long, narrow building (rather like a church, I suppose, though the thought did not cross my mind at the time) with forty (though it seemed like forty thousand) people inside. The counter was at the very far end. I was going to have to go down the length of the aisle. My only hope was not to be noticed through the great cloud of cigarette smoke, and the lively hubbub of conversation. However, as I walked the length of the shop I could feel all eyes turning on me. A wave of silence, like the wake of a ship followed me down to the counter. By the time I got there the silence was total.

I could hear the phoniness in my voice as I said just what you would expect some guilty vicar, coming to place a quick bet, would say: 'There is a man outside in a disabled person's car, who has asked me to place this bet for him.' I felt so false I did not really believe what I was saying myself. I was sure that my new 'congregation' did not.

As I walked back to the door a wave of laughter, and tittering, swept me from the place.

I had moved out — into the world where many

are at home. It was a dramatic sign to me of the dis-comfort and dis-ease we must be ready for if we are to participate in the mission of Christ to the world he entered at such cost.

That experience in the betting shop was to set me thinking.

I had no doubt which aisle I would rather walk down, or which one the people in that shop would rather be found in. There were two different worlds: and they were worlds apart. But was the gulf meant to be fixed, or could it be transcended? Surely this was why Jesus had come into our world; as holy God he touched the lives, and the bodies, of the sick, the outcasts, the lepers, and the prostitutes. He had come on the Father's mission, and the call to follow him was a call into that mission.

Little did I realise at the time that this experience was a preparation for the church's encounter with the inner-city youth culture of Sheffield.

Tense Company

Back in 1978 a young man, Chris Brain, had moved to Sheffield because his wife, Lynne, had just gained a place at the university to read music. Chris had come to faith a few years earlier and was concerned to apply his new-found faith to the rock scene he was already involved in and to the needs of society of which he was so aware. I quickly got to know Chris because he joined our fellowship group, and indeed, took over the leadership of it in due course from Ann and me.

Chris and Lynne were soon joined by other friends and, in 1981, formed themselves into a rock group, called initially Present Tense, but soon renamed simply Tense. They were a group open to God who had felt him calling them to take a different approach from that of the usual Christian rock group. 'Get out into the secular scene' was what they heard God telling them to do. There they attempted to work out the implications of their faith, rather than to become a Christian rock group producing directly evangelistic music.

The early years of Greenbelt, the writings of Jim Punton, and both David Watson and his rock-music-expert successor, Graham Cray, all had a formative influence on their thinking and lifestyle.

Tense was, in the best sense of the word, a struggling group. As the core of the group grew, they spent time in prayer, study and research about the full implications of the Christian faith to the culture they were involved with: a culture as distant from me and the church as that of the betting shop.

Searching

They were aware of two major strands in the social outworkings of the gospel that seemed to be the only two options available. On the right (politically, and theologically) was the Moral Majority of the United States. Strong on personal morality, it seemed to them to be more tied to the success culture of the Western world than to the teachings of scripture. The other strand was liberation theology, coming from Latin America, and expressing a largely Marxist interpretation of social problems. Tense had more sympathy with this strand, yet it left them dissatisfied, and seeking for something more — if such existed.

Three things seemed to be more important to them in their search for an authentic expression of Christianity. First, was worship and the knowledge of God. They had known God in their own experience, and knew this to be the key to all their Christianity; yet they found that there was little point of connection between the church's use of music in its worship and the music they wrote, played and lived with.

Second, was the importance of human relationships: it was a non-negotiable element of the faith — living in love with fellow Christians. For this reason, they began to live in community, sharing their money equally between those of them who were earning and those who were not (but working for Tense).

Third, was the kingdom. Like the church, which had found such invigorating unity around the very concrete church extension project, they were wrestling with what the kingdom was all about. Every clear definition seemed to be a man-made caricature, and every full explanation ended in vagueness. Their starting point was the ministry of Jesus. There they saw things combined that were not being combined anywhere else so far as they knew. Jesus healed, and cast out demons, *and* cared for the poor and disadvantaged. Tense knew that they had better questions than they had answers.

They also had a name which exactly described the relation between them and the church, especially through the time of shaking. They too were going through a time of spiritual darkness and distance from God, and a time of leadership struggle. That sense of lostness in a dark period was affecting the whole church. However, there were strong walls of

mutual fear, threat, and suspicion. They felt a
cultural exclusion like I had in the betting shop.
There was a love-hate relationship with the church
which was mutual. There was an underlying respect
and trust, otherwise we would have parted company long before; but that respect was like the
ocean depths. It was hidden from view and a
complete contrast from the troubled seas above.
They continually seemed out of step with the rest of
the church and specifically refused to have anything
to do with the Billy Graham mission.

By 1985, eighteen of them were living in community, though in a number of houses. They had
changed their name to the Nairn Street Community
because one of their houses, and the church
building, was on that road. It was not easy to get
them to hear John Wimber when he came to speak
at the signs and wonders conference in the city hall
in the November of that year. 'Not another rich
American selling triumphalism' was their attitude.
But they came.

Conference Week

Steve Williams, who by now had stood down as
youth leader and was involved with the Nairn Street
Community, was one of the first to find God very
present. After one of the first sessions John
Wimber asked everyone to stand as he invited the
Holy Spirit to come and work. Steve, still suspicious, remained firmly in his seat. As John spoke of
specific gifts that the Holy Spirit was giving there
and then, Steve turned to those around him. He
was in the middle of a cynical remark about the
'hyping' of the atmosphere when the Holy Spirit

came in such power on him that he slumped in his seat, lost all sense of hearing, and experienced God taking him ('in the Spirit') into another room and telling Steve that now things were to be done God's way.

That was just the beginning. Having spent weeks persuading them to come, I then spent four days trying (totally unsuccessfully) to stop them getting all their friends and relatives smuggled into the building without tickets, all of which had been taken before the conference had begun. They too met with God in very evident ways.

For the whole group that Sheffield conference week was a profound event. They experienced a love and acceptance from the Vineyard teams that they had not been experiencing in St Thomas's. Through John Wimber's teaching about the kingdom they saw the beginning of how supernatural power *and* the radical demands of discipleship and care for the poor could be combined. They also experienced a time of repentance for personal sins. Above all, they found 'God confirming the word with signs following'. What they had been struggling with for five years came together in five days.

The change in them was evident, and they seemed to move into this new realm of God's action with greater ease and speed than the rest of us. It had a transforming effect on my relationship with them. God quickly dealt with my fears and suspicions of them as a group, and gave me confidence to trust that he was at work in them. Barriers fell away within days, though we had no idea what would be opened up as a result. We were very soon to find out.

Fireworks!

After the Sheffield conference the Vineyard teams went out to twenty-four locations all over the north of England. We held two meetings in Sheffield, one was mounted in the cathedral by the Sheffield house church, and one was based on St Thomas's. We held them on the same nights in the hope of containing the numbers we expected.

It was the last night, the Wednesday, that was the never-to-be-forgotten meeting. The previous evening had been bonfire night, though for us this was to be the night of fireworks. People were everywhere. When all the seats were taken I realised that people were still coming in. I went to the church entrance to see how many more there were. To my horror I saw a crowd queueing outside the church, across the patio, down the steps, across the churchyard, over a cul-de-sac, and down the side street! We later estimated that we had one thousand people crammed into the building. The atmosphere was electric — partly because so many people were there, and partly because there was such a sense of expectancy. In fact there was a mixture of spiritual awe and fleshly excitement. Some, who could only see the latter, sadly missed out on the former.

Steve Nicholson, a young Vineyard pastor from inner-city Chicago, spoke. Afterwards he invited the Holy Spirit to come; and he came in incredible power. The Nairn Street Community were right at the front of the dais, where I was also. Steve told all those who were experiencing the Holy Spirit on them in a definite physical way to stand up because God was wanting to anoint them for power evangelism. I found myself in the midst of a group of black-clad young people. When the Spirit came all heaven, and yes all hell, were let loose. Some were screaming in emotional release, at least one demonised person was set free, others were weeping for the pain of the city, and prophesying through their tears. Many were being knocked to the floor under the power of the Spirit. Bodies were falling all around me.

An Idea!

In one of those rare moments that I know God has spoken to me the thought 'God wants to add one or two hundred young people like these to the church in the near future' was in my head without my having put it there. Right then my mind was not on future possibilities, it had been focused on the present chaos all around me, when this idea arrived. My understanding of the phrase 'near future' was that it meant months rather than days or a year.

Within a week I also knew that our existing services could not be the means of reaching such an unchurched culture. We were in a missionary situation and would have to start from scratch. It was not easy, even for a church that had become accustomed to change, to adjust to such a radical development. Fears had to be faced, in the staff team and on the church council. What made it more difficult was that when pressed and asked 'what exactly is it going to be like?' I could give no coherent answer. We were going to have to experiment and find out. It is a tribute to all involved that agreement was harmoniously, though not always unanimously, reached. By Easter of the following year (1986) we were ready to launch the nine o'clock service, initially for a three-month experimental period.

Because the Nairn Street Community of eighteen people, of whom ten were in full-time employment, were mounting the service it was possible to put considerable human resources into the venture. From the start the whole operation was done with tremendous thoroughness and attention to detail. Every Friday all the equipment is moved in for the evening in order to rehearse for the Sunday evening. It is then moved out of the building again and stored. The same operation is repeated again on Sunday afternoon. After that final rehearsal the equipment is moved to the games hall before being moved back again after the evening service.

The 6.30pm Evening Service was the biggest of the day and, initially at least, there was some anxiety about time pressure. We decided it would do no harm to restrict the 6.30pm service to ninety minutes, with a commitment to reach the blessing by 8pm. However, after each of our services we now also have time to pray for people — often in response to words of knowledge about specific needs which are given during the course of the service.

I was certainly anxious that, although the leaders of the nine-o'clock service were mature and sensitive people, some of the enthusiastic young people who were involved with them might seek to 'move in' each Sunday evening in an aggressive or disruptive way. I need not have worried. They were a model of sensitive, efficient and patient work and the move has almost always gone without a hitch: even when, as occasionally happens — especially at major events like baptisms or confirmation — the earlier service runs late.

The whole operation is very well organised, and run much more like a business than a church. In my view that is a compliment, as the church seems so often to glory in its amateurishness.

Under Way

The brief was simple. The leaders were instructed to do 'exactly what the rest of the church does; namely to worship God, pray, read and teach from the scriptures, and to minister to the people'. However, they were given the freedom and authority to do it in any way they judged to be appropriate.

Just as we began to work on the implications of such a venture the important Church of England report *Faith in the City* was launched. Its concern with the state, and the people, of the inner city was a great encouragement to us. Our concern was to reach the urban youth culture to which the report gave much attention. The all-too-short section on worship (p134f) was particularly helpful in encouraging us to experiment with a new style and pattern that would reflect and reach a new cultural grouping.

To date that has involved writing all their own music in what could be described as a 'rock idiom', using very subdued (some say 'non-existent') lighting. After the sheer volume of the music the most striking thing about the service to the initial observer is the dramatic use of visuals. Nine slide projectors are used to cover the walls with graphic images — usually not particularly obvious in their meaning, to me at least! It is a striking setting, and really an electronic-age form of stained glass windows.

One that stands out in my mind was the use of a picture of massed ranks of Chinese athletes wearing nothing but white loin cloths. The view was looking across the diagonal lines of serried ranks. The slide had been reproduced nine times so that each projector was projecting the same picture. The worshipper was encased in a goldfish bowl of humanity. It had a striking effect. The service has also made use of a video team to make short reports and films which are then used in the service.

Interestingly the service is not only the noisiest of all (a good number of the congregation accompanying parts of the worship on their whistles), it is also the quietest, with periods of meditation. I find it the most demanding, and the most responsive, of our four congregations to preach to. It has been necessary to be open to the leaders of the service for instruction in how to preach in such a setting. That has been an experience itself.

The first such service attracted sixty people, about forty of whom had previously been regular worshippers at the other services. Within eighteen months those 'one or two hundred young people' had been added to the church. Indeed by the summer of 1988 we had nearly four hundred people a Sunday.

Seeing several hundred unconventionally dressed young people making their way to church is itself quite a sight, and a great joy. It has certainly changed my attitude to the urban youth culture. Previous to the nine o'clock service I would be fearful of such people. I now relate much more easily to them, not least because when I meet such young people in town, as likely as not, they will be members of my church.

Some people feared, as we launched into the nine o'clock service, that, especially with the use of the rock idiom, it would be entertainment. I was telling one member of the church how efficiently they moved their sixteen thousand pounds worth of equipment into position after the end of the 6.30pm service. 'That just proves it's only entertainment, doesn't it?' they said very aggressively. I asked why. 'Needing sixteen thousand pounds worth of equipment for worship' they stated, in a tone of voice which suggested the fact itself made the point 'Wait a minute,' I replied, 'do you know how much our new organ cost? Sixteen thousand pounds!' For all of us it has been a stretching cultural adjustment to be part of a church which includes 'the nine o'clockers'.

Making Disciples

It is important to say that this is not just a worship phenomena. It is also an expression of those other two values that were established in the Tense company; namely, relationships and the work of the kingdom.

All those who come to the service and are wanting to take discipleship seriously are assigned to one of the discipleship groups (the equivalent of supporting fellowships). Entry into them is by no means automatic. Each potential member is interviewed before they are allowed to join. Several matters are checked out with them, and where necessary action is taken, before they join a group.

First, it is established that they have come to a place of repentance and faith before God, and have been prayed for to know the power of the Holy Spirit in their lives. The cost of discipleship is then explained, and in particular the implications of being involved in some form of service (whether internal to the nine-o'clock service, or part of its outreach to other young people). Finally, potential discipleship group members are helped to face issues of discipleship in particular relation to sexual matters, and as far as money is concerned. In both areas a new member would be helped to deal with the past so that their membership of the church can truly be a new beginning.

These specific matters are faced in the nine o'clock service, not because sex and sexuality are more important to challenge than, say, materialism, but because in this particular congregation they are often the dominant idols and secular values which the kingdom of God challenges.

Members of the discipleship groups are part of what is called the 'seventy-two'. The title is taken from the sending out of that number of people by Jesus as recorded in the gospels. It points to the sense of active service which is to be the mentality of all Christians; and to the call of God, in Jesus, for every believer to be a disciplined 'soldier and servant of Christ until our life's end'. The feel of the congregation is one of joyful and whole-hearted commitment to Christ; caring and gentle love and concern for all those who come, and unashamed willingness to be part of a disciplined group that is seeking to bring in the kingdom of God.

There is a strong emphasis not only on the healing ministry and on 'power evangelism', but

also on service to the poor. The whole venture is
built around establishing an outworking of the
kingdom of God in the urban youth culture.
Members of the congregation, including leaders,
are now involved in night shelters for homeless
teenagers and single men, women's refuges and
rehabilitation centres for people coming off drugs.

God's power has been evident throughout this
venture. Close on two hundred young people have
now been converted to faith in Christ. Of these,
over half are unemployed. We have seen well over
fifty such people stop taking drugs; for some that
involved freedom from heroin. A staggering forty
to fifty per cent of all the women who have come to
faith have at sometime in their life experienced
rape or sexual abuse. Many are from broken homes
and have experienced God rebuilding them as
people. These are young people with no previous
church background. Indeed they are from a culture
that can accurately be described as being unchurched.

No publicity material has been produced at any
stage in the life of the nine o'clock service. The
whole venture depends entirely on those involved
telling others of their faith, and bringing them
along. The problem has never been 'how can we get
people to church?', but always 'how can we contain
growth so that the whole venture does not fail
because of a too rapid numerical growth?' Keeping
up with that growth has always been the problem.
So, for example, having started, in effect, with one
discipleship group in April 1986, the twentieth one
was started within two years. When the vast
majority have no church background that repres-
ents a very fast rate of training.

Integration

It has only been possible to come so far, and so fast, as a result of much patience, struggle, and sheer hard work. It has not all been plain sailing.

We have not always been able to balance vibrant worship with happy neighbours. As a result of noise complaints from neighbours, we have had the environmental health officer coming round during church service time to check the decibel-level readings outside. When that happened I was reminded of the line from the old hymn 'The church with psalms must shout / no door can keep them out'! A half-page article about the service appeared in the *Sheffield Star* under the caption 'Give me that high decibel religion!' Sometimes the fault has been ours.

Chief among our struggles has been the integration of the existing church with NOS (short for nine o'clock service). It has been hard work on both sides.

The leaders of NOS were much clearer in their minds about the implications of starting a new service; we had seen little beyond something new happening at nine o'clock on Sunday evenings. Quickly we seemed to be in a situation where a separate church with an entirely independent life, structure and organisation (complete with its own office) was emerging. Old fears, suspicions, and distrust re-surfaced and had to be dealt with.

I certainly had little idea of what we were doing in launching such a service. Around the world I now hear stories of such ventures that have eventually despaired of the church and gone off to form a separate group. Both sides are committed to not doing so here. We know we need each other, and that our ability to live and work and worship together, across cultural barriers, is itself an important sign of the kingdom.

It has meant endless hours of meetings. Sometimes it has felt like riding a bicycle through treacle. Yet we remain not only together, but committed to making major adjustments on both sides in order for the kingdom to come through our oneness in the faith.

Seeing Ahead

On a good day the future of the nine o'clock service looks very exciting. On a bad day I wonder what on earth I have got myself into. Leaving home at five o'clock on a Sunday afternoon to prepare myself for the 6.30pm service, and not getting home to close on 11pm, proved to be a punishing schedule. One Sunday, early in the new venture, I came home and promptly fainted. We have had to adjust to more reasonable schedules.

Conservative estimates indicate that we could well be handling a congregation of over one thousand such young people within a couple of years. They have already grown too big for our building although we have found no evident solution to that problem as yet. There is much work yet to do on such matters as introducing the sacraments to the worship, and developing the ministry to those in need in the city. I sense that what could be happening is that a twentieth-century Lindisfarne, with a rich community life yet committed to going out on teaching and healing missions, may be in the making. We are far from ready for such a work.

The set of circumstances that brought about this service have been quite unique, and evidently another part of God's agenda for St Thomas's. Yet we long to see this culture being reached with the gospel in many other cities, and in ways unique to those places. How that might happen we cannot see, but with the Nairn Street Community able to release seven people full-time there is a tremendous growth potential which we continue to both marvel at, and keep running fast to catch up with.

Chapter Thirteen

SIGNPOSTS

The combined effect of moving into congregations, and developing the nine o'clock service, has led us both to look back with thankfulness and forward with eager (even if slightly nervous) anticipation.

The nature of the story that has been told makes the future impossible to predict, beyond the words of that classic newspaper headline 'Great surprise expected!' We have continually been discovering that God has plans for us as individuals, and for his church, that we could never have predicted. We have learnt to keep open to him and to the way that he wishes to take his church. It is, after all, *his* church. He is the one who has died for it, and has brought it forgiveness through the cross.

Looking back, the growth of the church has been an exciting, as well as disturbing, journey of discovery. We have come face to face with both our human frailty, and also the amazing grace of God to see his people through to the next step he has for them. We did not set out with a clear map of where we were going but rather, as we went, we came across various principles which were like signposts for us, to show us the next stage of that journey.

However, we have learnt some lessons about

how to stay open to God and be available to him.

1 Discovering God's Agenda

There are two crucial parts to the commissioning of
the disciples by the risen Lord as recorded in the
opening chapter of the Acts of the Apostles.

First, is the promise of the Spirit: 'You will
receive power when the Holy Spirit comes upon
you.' Without that divine empowering none of the
rest of the story could have taken place.

The second part of the sending out of the apostles
is the description of the work that lay ahead. 'You
will be my witnesses in Jerusalem, Judea, and
Samaria, and to the ends of the earth' (Acts 1.8).
Without that divine agenda the story makes little
sense; for what follows seems like a random series
of unconnected events. There are joys, and times of
great effectiveness, interspersed with tragedy, such
as the deaths of Stephen and James. There are
great struggles too. They come initially from the
persecution by Paul, and then are evident in his
own subsequent, and highly troubled, labours.
There are squabbles that so often mar all human
social activity; arguments about the distribution of
food to the widows, and conflict between leaders
about whether Mark can be taken on mission.
Mysteriously the story ends with the major character in the story, the apostle Paul, under house arrest
in Rome. The story seems so full of crisis, conflict
and unpredictable events that the reader is left
wondering what sense to make of it all.

Yet, at the end we can look and see that God's
original plan has been fulfilled. God's agenda
enables us to understand what is happening, and to

see where the story is going. It is set down at the
beginning as a signpost. It can be picked up, even if
with difficulty, as the story proceeds. What matters
most, after twenty-eight chapters of tragedy and
triumph, is that in the end we can look back across
all the struggle, and puzzle of events, and see that
the gospel had been taken to 'Jerusalem, Judea,
and Samaria and the ends of the earth'. God has
been working his purposes out in the midst of very
mixed human fortunes. God had both written, and
fulfilled, his agenda.

The story of St Thomas's, over the 1970s in
particular, followed a similar pattern. For those of
us involved, we were simply responding to the
varied kaleidoscope of events that were passing
before us. Only as we looked back did we see the
pattern and purpose. First had come personal
renewal of faith. Out of that came the renewal of
our relationships, and from that had come the
re-ordering of our buildings. It all looked so neat,
and tidy, and logical. It suggested that we were
working to some well-thought-out programme and
plan for the development of the church.

We were, of course; but it was not ours! We have
seen the same pattern in the 1980s. There was no
way in which we could have predicted, let alone
planned the idea of a local ecumenical project, or
the rediscovery of the supernatural dimension, a
time of shaking, the movement into congregations,
or the establishing of a nine-o'clock service. God
was continuing to spring upon us his surprises.

'The Son does nothing of his own accord, only
what he sees the Father doing' (John 5.19) was
continuing to prove a vital scripture to steer by. A
passage from Tom Smail's book *The Forgotten*

Father crystallised this principle for me around this time. He points out how working on God's agenda was written deep into the fabric of Jesus' whole being. Tom Smail writes:

> Every action of Jesus originates and is directed by and towards the person, purpose and glory of the Father. It is from first to last *obedient* action, not initiating or innovating, but rather discerning and following. This is not a limitation on its spontaneity and freedom, but rather the source of it, because it is always personal response within a relationship and never external conformity to impersonal rule or regulation.

This principle of seeking to discover God's will and God's agenda has driven us back time and time again, to prayer, to reflection, and to study of the scriptures. We have learnt not to trust man-made plans and ideas, but rather to have good confidence in the, sometimes strange, ways in which God leads his people. It has meant that many of us have had to set aside our plans, and ideas, and to wait patiently for God's. In the process it has brought us together as unitedly we seek God's way whether it confirms or contradicts our hopes.

2   Breaking Out of the Club Mentality

One of the first things we had to face in working for the growth of the church was the resistance within the church itself to anything so uncomfortable. I was aware, from research done by the Urban Church Project and other groups, that the most usual cause for a church not to grow has nothing to do with the hardness of heart of the unbelieving world around us. It has to do with the reluctance of the church to change.

Human selfishness always pulls away from the disturbing frontier work of making Christ known in an unbelieving world, into something more comfortable. We want to change the church-for-others, into a club-for-us. It happens in a multitude of ways.

It happens in our worship. We become familiar with the way things have always been done, and cannot understand or have patience with, those newcomers who find things difficult. I heard a story of a family who were once moved to seek after God together. They turned up at their local church one Sunday. Assuming the place was like any other meeting place they went straight to the front and sat down. When the service began they realised to their horror that there were seven rows of empty seats between them and the rest of the congregation, who were sitting in the back half of the church. The vicar announced the first hymn. The family stood up, only to discover that the congregation remained seated whilst the organist played the opening bars of the music. So the family sat down, with embarrassment. At just the moment they did so, the congregation stood up! Hungry for God, yet covered in confusion, they never darkened the doors of that church again.

It was for just this reason that we stopped chanting the psalms, because we could not in all conscience feel it right to say to the newcomer (by our actions): 'To become a Christian you need not only to come in repentance and faith to Jesus Christ as Lord, but also you need to learn a fourteenth-century way of singing — indeed you need to learn that first before you can hear the other part.' That does not mean that we have sought to take all the mystery out of our services. There is a world of difference between the mystery of worship and old-fashioned habits.

All the time we have given attention to how the newcomer feels. We announce page numbers (or have them up on the overhead projector). We use service booklets not the ASB in full as it is far too daunting to most people. We speak in our normal voices, and use as little 'language of Zion' as is possible. We subscribe to the statement of James Philip in his little booklet *Christian Maturity*, when he says, 'Salvation is essentially considered the restoration of humanity to man.' He goes on to say, 'It cannot be too strongly emphasised that if spiritual considerations overlay our lives with un-naturalness, something terrible has happened, and we must at all costs break through it.'

But the club mentality shows itself in deeper ways. *It appears every time we make decisions without thought for the newcomer.* It makes me sad to see churches that have, often over a long period, chosen that way and then regretted it when it is too late. The picture comes to my mind of a couple who chose, when newly married, not to have children; and then in their later years lived to regret the decision. It was the easiest and most comfortable thing to do *then,* but *now* there is regret in old age that there are no grandchildren to enjoy, and no future generation to pass on either their values or their valuables to. Many churches are like that. Years ago they made decisions for their comfort. Churches like that now find they have no one below pensionable age and are becoming increasingly neurotic about how the younger generation have

rejected religion. The truth is that they themselves
have closed the doors long ago on the next
generation. Lovingly we have to help such churches
come to terms with their terminal state. More
important, is the need for us to ensure that we
never do that in our day.

The 'car park full' mentality is another way that
we turn the church-for-others, into a club-for-us.
This particular malaise happens to growing churches, which is why it is so dangerous. The fact that
such churches are growing masks the other fact that
they are committed to limited growth. Our goal, at
St Thomas's, is not just to *fill the church with
believers,* but to *empty the parish of unbelievers.*
However, some growing churches only have a
vision for filling the church. When that is achieved
the sense of arrival sets in and the church begins to
turn into a club. The Church Growth Movement is
so right when it says that the most dangerous place
for any church to be is full.

Resistance to newcomers is another way in which
the club mentality expresses itself. Visiting a church
as rural dean once I was told by the PCC, who were
concerned about the lack of newcomers, 'We are a
very friendly church.' Visiting the church later I saw
the truth — and error — of what was said. Among
the 'in' group they were very friendly. The trouble
was no newcomer could find the way in.

One thing that we have emphasised continually
at St Thomas's, is that when we come to church we
come to worship and to welcome. We encourage
everyone who has been in the church for four weeks
or more to consider themselves 'pastor-to-the-pew'
in which they are sitting. In that way we are all
involved in welcoming the visitor or newcomer. We

learnt to do this even when it lands us in embarrassing situations.

One member of the church who had clearly got this message made sure that the newcomer sitting next to him, a gentleman in his middle sixties, did not lose his place in the Alternative Service booklet for Rite A communion. Several times he was shown the correct page.

He spoke to me afterwards and was obviously impressed. However, it had not actually been necessary because he was Bishop Gordon Arthur, who had actually chaired the Liturgical Commission of Australia in the writing of its new liturgy. He was quite familiar with ours!

Bound up with this concern for the outsider has been, for me, a willingness to learn from the secular world. Part of the cause of the decline of Christianity in the West has been our loss of nerve. The result has been a church, and a leadership, more committed to keeping everyone happy than to breaking new ground. We can learn from those who have not lost their nerve — such as industry and the armed forces. The tragedy is the church often does not have real faith in its 'product' (the gospel), or take seriously the battle. We can learn much from the military about leadership structures because they depend on them to survive. Much of the Christian church is not too concerned even about survival. We can learn much from business about effective organisation, but are often more interested in comfort than effectiveness.

3   Church Growth is a Co-operative

A remark by the then Bishop of Manchester, at the
service to mark the opening of the new hall at Holy
Trinity, Platt, Manchester, has always stuck in my
mind. 'You have worked,' he said, 'as if there is no
such thing as prayer; and have prayed as if there is
no such thing as work.' It summed up so much that
I learnt at that time, and has remained with me over
the years. It expresses well the mystery of the
kingdom of God. We lapse, at our peril, to one side
of the equation whenever we act, out of unbelief, as
though it all depended on our efforts. We also go
contrary to God's purposes when, with a false and
super-spiritual attitude, we think we have no
responsibility because it is all up to God.

One passage of scripture has spoken to me
deeply over the years about this amazing privilege
we have of co-operating with God. It is the
shortest, and one of my favourite, parables:

> This is what the kingdom of God is like. A man
> scatters seed on the ground. Night and day, whether
> he sleeps or gets up, the seed sprouts and grows,
> though he does not know how. All by itself the soil
> produces the corn — first the stalk, then the ear, then
> the full grain in the ear. As soon as the grain is ripe,
> he puts the sickle to it, because the harvest has come.
> (Mark 4.26-29)

Notice that the kingdom is not the seed, or the
growth, or the man, or the harvest, but the whole
event. Notice moreover that what is happening is
taking place on two different levels and that Jesus is
drawing attention to the distinction between them.
He is also teaching the importance of both levels of

activity. There is the level of nature where the most vital thing is taking place — growth. The effects of sun, and rain, and the action of the soil, combined with the germinating power placed within the seed are all happening outside of the man's control. Jesus draws attention to the farmer's powerlessness: it does not matter what he does — 'whether he sleeps or gets up' — no amount of effort or anxiety will make any difference. And yet, he is as essential as are the natural forces if there is to be a harvest. The farmer must sow the seed, see the ripe moment, put in the sickle, and gather in the harvest. This is the other level, the human one; it is as essential as the other level. The kingdom of God happens as God finds men and women committed to full co-operation with him.

So it is with church growth. There are two levels on which things are taking place. Church growth takes place when God creates and when also, at the same time, *we cultivate.* We need to be clear about what God alone can and will do, as we also need to know what our part is. We cannot create growth. Our calling is to cry out to God in prayer for him to work the kingdom among us and to give that growth. However, once that happens we have a job. God expects us to gather and care for the harvest; to provide the circumstances in which that growth can be sustained and multiplied.

This is the point at which I find myself uncomfortable with the Church Growth Movement. Stemming from Fuller Seminary in California, this strand in Christian thinking about mission has sought to analyse what causes churches to grow, and what frustrates that growth. I have a great respect for many of its leaders and have learnt much from the movement. They are saying many things that the church urgently needs to hear. And yet I have always felt the need to hold back from wholehearted agreement at one crucial point. In the final issue what I hear the movement saying is 'do these ten (or however many) things and the church will grow'. There is not a proper distinction between divine creativity and human industry, or a proper recognition of their interaction. Yet it is this that makes church growth such a wonderful adventure with God.

Another way of putting this is to say I have found that *church growth is an art not a science.* A science is mechanical, complete in itself, which it is proper for us to seek to master and control. An art is a skill of co-operation with our environment; whether the paint of the artist, the humidity in which the bowler seeks to spin the cricket ball, or the words used by a poet. For an artist there is constant discovery in the skill of co-operating with something that is never totally in our control.

Once having grasped this co-operative nature of church growth, two things happened. First, the importance of discovering God's agenda, especially in prayer, became much more vital. Indeed that is the most important thing in the whole operation.

However, it also heightened the need to get our structures and management right, because that is the task that God has given to us. I have often had to cope with being labelled 'a good administrator', which — in Christian circles — is often a way of damning with faint praise. Yet, I am convinced that it is crucial to bringing in the kingdom. Winning people to faith, without having the resources and structures to help them to continue and grow in that faith is dishonouring to God, and tragic for those people. Working on those structures is crucial to the growth of the church.

4   Changing as You Grow

An important principle that I have learnt from both actual experience, and from considering lessons from industry, is that as a venture grows it needs to change the whole nature of how it works. A small family business employing all five members of the family hardly needs an 'in-house' news-sheet, but many large firms find such means of communication essential for harmony and success.

We have had to learn to change to cope with the different size of the church. Indeed, we have had to learn that change is often needed before further growth can take place.

The first, and most important, change comes at around the level of one hundred and fifty members. Significantly most churches grow to that size, and then cease to grow further. In the Anglican parochial system it is interesting to note that this happens irrespective of whether the parish has a population of two thousand or twelve thousand or twenty-two thousand. The internal structure of the church is fully stretched; no further growth can take place. The normal church structure depends on the relationship between the leader and the members. One hundred and fifty to two hundred people is about as many as any one person can get to know. Once you add fifty people to that number by *mission,* you tend to loose another fifty people by *omission.* It is then that you hear remarks like 'He doesn't seem to be interested in us older folk any more', 'The place is just not the same', and similar such thoughts. This will always happen unless we can find a way to change how the church operates.

There was a particularly crucial time when I had to face this, and was so glad to have the support of David Hughes. I realised that I had to abandon the idea of knowing everyone who comes to church. My role was changing from caring for everyone to ensuring that everyone was cared for. It was not easy for me or the church. It felt like abandoning the pastoral calling that was laid on me. In reality it was multiplication of it. In this situation David preached about how Moses took Jethro's advice in delegating responsibility. He then pointed out that only the hard cases came to Moses. 'Gone are the days,' David added by way of application, 'when a visit by Robert was a sign of honour: now it is evidence that everyone else despairs of sorting you out, and Robert is coming — as a last resort.' The point was deliberately overstated, but the message was lastingly received.

Another way in which growth has affected how we operate as a church is in the way we welcome and seek to integrate newcomers. As a smaller church we could leave it to individuals. Everyone knew who the newcomers were, and people took the responsibility to welcome them, and to join them into a fellowship group. By the time we had reached six hundred worshippers often even the clergy did not know who the newcomers were. We had to change the way we operated. We now have a welcome pastor and a welcome team in each congregation whose sole task in the life of the church is to spot, befriend, and help newcomers to move into the life of the church as quickly as

possible. They even have a check list of the eight
points of welcome to help them find where people
are at in their faith, and how we can best help.

5   Releasing Constraints

In any situation there are balancing forces: some
working for growth, others for stability. This is true
in a church. Some people will be working for
growth, development, change; and others will be
working for stability, order, and the upholding of
tradition. It is important not only to recognise this,
but also to know how to handle them in such a way
that growth can take place.

The most obvious course where growth is not
taking place is to try to strengthen the hand of those
people and those forces working for growth.
However, this can all too easily be counter-
productive. Growth is seen, and felt, to be a threat
by those who are concerned not to rock the boat.
An emphasis on growth may well therefore create
'an equal and opposite reaction'. Sadly the forces of
reaction often have won the day in the life of the
Christian church.

A more effective way is usually to ease the
pressure on the forces pulling against growth rather
than to push hard on the positive factors. For
example, in the area of evangelism, we all too easily
look for ways of putting pressure on everyone in the
church to bring friends and neighbours, relatives
and colleagues at work, to faith — or at least to
church. The result is often a deepening sense of
guilt, rather than a harvest of souls. A more
creative way would be to ask what the constraints
are. Discovering why people do not tell others of

their faith, and finding out how to remove that
obstacle can be a much more creative way through
the problem.

This has been the underlying pattern of the
growth of St Thomas's. Each step forward has come
as a result of our getting stuck, and finding growth
levelling off. Rather than berating the church for
not doing better, we have sought — by a mixture of
prayer and thorough analysis — to identify what the
obstacle is and then to remove it. It is all part of the
process of working on the basis of grace (giving/
resourcing) rather than works (demand/moral
pressure).

I inherited a growing church, yet one in which
also the growth was tailing off. Rather than apply
moral pressure to try harder, I sought to discover
what the block was. Disturbingly I found that the
block was in me: a lack of reality in what I had to
tell. Out of that seeking came renewal to me and
the church. When growth had taken place through
renewal and the development of fellowship groups
we discovered that our buildings were a major
obstacle, and sought to release that constraint
through the building project. The same problem,
lack of space, occurred again ten years later. The
development of congregations has been the way we
have released the constraint this time, and so on...

One of the great advantages of this approach is
that it tends to solve underlying problems, rather
than to add inefficient solutions on top of a problem
that has not been solved. Telling people they
should be sharing their faith more when they have
no confidence in the faith they do have will only
add guilt to doubt. That will not motivate anyone.
Telling people they ought to give more, when they

have no vision to be motivated to give, is likely to add resistance to lack of enthusiasm. There is not likely to be much giving in that atmosphere.

Best of all, this approach has a unifying effect. Those who are resistant feel they are being listened to. Those who are keen address themselves to the problems that others feel. Communication and co-operative working on real problems replace sterile arguments about whether we are all called to be evangelists or not, or whether we should tithe, and if so, is it before or after tax!

So one of the most creative, liberating, and unifying questions that can be asked in the face of failure, problems and lack of success, is 'what are the constraints in this situation?' Then we can start to seek ways to release them. Rather than asking 'how can we get them to…?' questions, we need to be asking 'what are the factors working against this move…?' Then we will see movement.

6   Death and Resurrection

It was out of this discovery about the place of the negatives that a deeper truth was dawning on me. Fundamental to our experience of growth at St Thomas's has been the pattern of death and resurrection. Growth, blessing, yes even that much feared word success have come about again and again through the church's willingness to go the way of the Cross.

Becoming involved in renewal was risky business. There were plenty of stories of churches that had been damaged and divided by such a step. However, the church heard the call of God and was willing to go that way. Out of the personal shaking, and tensions within the fellowship, we came through to blessing for the whole church. It was risk, pain, conflict, misunderstanding first, *then* blessing, joy, and growth. Through death to resurrection.

The building project took us along a similar path. There was enormous risk. We launched into it in poverty. The final bill was two-thirds of a million pounds. We began with one thousand pounds in the bank. Time and time again, we took two steps forward and the target moved two steps away. It was a difficult way. It was a venture of faith, but faith functions where you have no sight of the things hoped for. It is simply the God-given ability to hold on when things are desperate.

Another aspect of death and resurrection is the willingness to go back to places where we have made mistakes to tackle the problem again. The development of congregations was the fruit of our having tried 'areas'. When we abandoned them it would have been easier to forget that whole problem of the middle-sized grouping. However, we found the courage to face the same problem again. It was through doing so that congregations emerged.

Christians are plagued today by two false options that block our path. On the one hand is a poverty mentality that rejoices in our amateurism, finds comfort in a remnant theology, and attempts to turn the Cross into justification for failing. On the other hand there is the prosperity gospel that offers a slick and worldly success geared to the materialistic culture around us. What Jesus has given us in his ministry, especially in his passion, is a life-giving pattern. As we face and go through weaknesses, poverty, failure, hostility, misunderstanding, and naked physical and spiritual attack, *there* we will meet with God and his blessing. The fruit that is borne is flavoured by grace and humility rather than soured by human achievement.

As a church we were led into what I call the *Easter Eve syndrome*. By this I mean that there has not only to be the death of something before new life can appear, but usually there needs to be a period in between the old and the new. Rarely can you immediately know the right replacement. It is so much easier, when stopping something, to announce the new alternative. Our experience has been that we have had to find the faith to stop something with no clear understanding of what, if anything, might replace it. Part of the reason, as I now understand it, is that God intends the vacuum to drive us to seek his ways afresh.

In practically every area of ministry which died in the mid-1970s, after a period of vacuum, a new work has emerged which has touched a wider circle of people than the one it replaced. Where once we had uniformed organisations for one aspect of youth work, we now have a full-time youth worker overseeing a much wider range of activities. Where once we had a robed choir we now have a number of worship teams assisting the worship not only in a way more appropriate to the needs of the church at the end of the twentieth century, but also helping us in fellowship groups, at the central prayer meeting, and in other ways to make worship our first concern. God has been giving back 'in good measure, pressed down, and overflowing', what we have been willing to let die.

7   It's All Done by Grace

One of the questions I least like being asked is: 'To what do you attribute the growth of St Thomas's?'

It is not an easy question to answer because I have come to the conclusion that like baking a good cake, or creating a happy family, there are a whole series of ingredients delicately balanced together. There is no one simple technique.

The only one sentence answer I do have is: *'It's all done by grace.'* Theologically that certainly fits with the gospel. It is the golden thread that draws together many of the principles I have outlined from our experience. *Discovering God's agenda* involves our recognising that he has a plan for the growth of the church which we need to receive from him, rather than attempt to achieve it for him. *Church growth as a co-operative* points to the fact that, like the farmer, we are only stewards of something that has an inherent growth dynamic if only the environment can be made sufficiently sympathetic to that growth. We can no more create the growth of the church than we can create the growth of a cabbage. Our task is simply to provide the setting in which that growth can be realised.

Breaking out of the club-mentality is a response to experiencing the giving of God in such a way that we are motivated to give to others and not close the door on them. *Releasing the constraints* has to do with letting life out rather than attempting to create or achieve it. Above all, it is the grace of God made available to man through the *death and resurrection* of Jesus that provides the growth dynamic of the church. It is his grace which is the germinating power of the kingdom at work in the world today.

Of all the signposts, this principle of grace is — I believe — the single most important guide in helping the church steer its way through the problems and into the blessings that God has in store for it in his purposes of love.

APPENDIX ONE
BUILDING PROJECT FINANCES

1 INCOME AND EXPENDITURE TOTALS BY YEARS

As at Dec 31	Yearly Income £	Accumulated Income £	Accumulated Expenditure £
1975	1,978	1,978	—
1976	12,180	14,158	—
1977	36,434	50,592	—
1978	85,969	136,561	9,578
1979	131,790	268,351	131,920
1980	296,854	565,205	479,003
1981	44,557	609,762	603,067
1982/3	26,737	636,499	636,499

2 APPROXIMATE INCOME CATEGORIES

	%	£
Direct giving by church family	52	330,979
Income Tax rebates	15	95,475
Gifts from Trust Funds	16	101,840
Capital Item Sales	5	31,825
Gifts from friends of church	4	25,460
Interest on Short Term Deposit balances	8	50,920
	100	636,499

3 TOTAL COST ESTIMATES

	£
July 1977	250,000
October 1977	275,000
August 1978	409,326
April 1979 (Tender Price)	486,760
September 1979	525,000
December 1979	564,282
February 1980	572,998
April 1980	578,285
August 1980	588,688
October 1980	597,426
Final cost	**636,499**

APPENDIX TWO

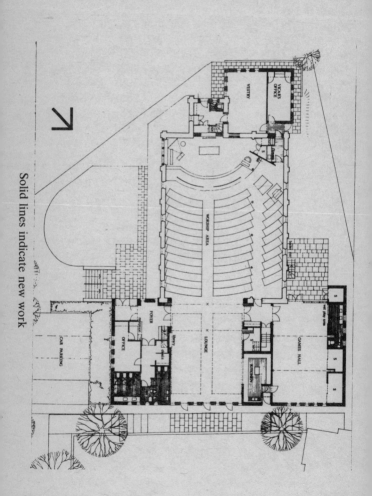

Solid lines indicate new work